THE
WORLD

Out of Control

How it
will end...

E.G. White

D1370626

 Remnant
Publications

Coldwater MI 49036
www.remnantpublications.com

Published by
Remnant Publications
649 East Chicago Road
Coldwater MI 49036
517-279-1304
www.remnantpublications.com

This book is a portion of a work originally published
under the title, *The Great Controversy.*

All Bible Scripture is taken from the King James Version.

Cover design by David Berthiaume
Text design by Greg Solie • AltamontGraphics.com

ISBN 978-1-933291-38-3

Contents

One

—The Destruction of Jerusalem—

"If thou hadst known, even thou, at least in this thy day, the things which belong unto thy peace! but now they are hid from thine eyes. For the days shall come upon thee, that thine enemies shall cast a trench about thee, and compass thee round, and keep thee in on every side, and shall lay thee even with the ground, and thy children within thee; and they shall not leave in thee one stone upon another; because thou knewest not the time of thy visitation." Luke 19:42-44.

From the crest of Olivet, Jesus looked upon Jerusalem. Fair and peaceful was the scene spread out before Him. It was the season of the Passover, and from all lands the children of Jacob had gathered there to celebrate the great national festival. In the midst of gardens and vineyards, and green slopes studded with pilgrims' tents, rose the terraced hills, the stately palaces, and massive bulwarks of Israel's capital. The daughter of Zion seemed in her pride to say, I sit a queen and shall see no sorrow; as lovely then, and deeming herself as secure in Heaven's favor, as when, ages before, the royal minstrel sang: "Beautiful for situation, the joy of the whole earth, is Mount Zion, ... the city of the great King." Psalm 48:2. In full view were the magnificent buildings of the temple. The rays of the setting sun lighted up the snowy whiteness of its marble walls and gleamed from golden gate and tower and pinnacle. "The perfection of beauty" it stood, the pride of the Jewish nation. What child of Israel could gaze upon the scene without a thrill of joy and admiration! But far other thoughts occupied the mind of Jesus. "When He was come near, He beheld the city, and wept over it." Luke 19:41. Amid the universal rejoicing of the triumphal entry, while palm branches waved, while glad hosannas awoke the echoes of the hills, and thousands of voices declared Him king, the world's Redeemer was overwhelmed with a sudden and mysterious sorrow. He, the Son of God, the Promised One of Israel, whose power had conquered death and called its captives from the grave, was in tears, not of ordinary grief, but of intense, irrepressible agony.

His tears were not for Himself, though He well knew whither His feet were tending. Before Him lay Gethsemane, the scene of His approaching agony. The sheepgate also was in sight, through which for centuries the victims for sacrifice had been led, and which was to open for Him when He should be "brought as a lamb to the slaughter." Isaiah 53:7. Not far distant was Calvary, the place of crucifixion. Upon the path which Christ was soon to tread must fall the horror of great darkness as He should make His soul an offering for sin. Yet it was not the contemplation of these scenes that cast the shadow upon Him in this hour of gladness. No foreboding of His own superhuman anguish clouded that unselfish spirit. He wept for the doomed thousands of Jerusalem—because of the blindness and impenitence of those whom He came to bless and to save.

The history of more than a thousand years of God's special favor and guardian care, manifested to the chosen people, was open to the eye of Jesus. There was Mount Moriah, where the son of promise, an unresisting victim, had been bound to the altar—emblem of the offering of the Son of God. There the covenant of blessing, the glorious Messianic promise, had been confirmed to the father of the faithful. Genesis 22:9, 16-18. There the flames of the sacrifice ascending to heaven from the threshing floor of Ornan had turned aside the sword of the destroying angel (1 Chronicles 21)—fitting symbol of the Saviour's sacrifice and mediation for guilty men. Jerusalem had been honored of God above all the earth. The Lord had "chosen Zion," He had "desired it for His habitation." Psalm 132:13. There, for ages, holy prophets had uttered their messages of warning. There priests had waved their censers, and the cloud of incense, with the prayers of the worshipers, had ascended before God. There daily the blood of slain lambs had been offered, pointing forward to the Lamb of God. There Jehovah had revealed His presence in the cloud of glory above the mercy seat. There rested the base of that mystic ladder connecting earth with heaven (Genesis 28:12; John 1:51)—that ladder upon which angels of God descended and ascended, and which opened to the world the way into the holiest of all. Had Israel as a nation preserved her allegiance to Heaven, Jerusalem would have stood forever, the elect of God. Jeremiah 17:21-25. But the history of that favored people was a record of backsliding and rebellion. They had resisted Heaven's grace, abused their privileges, and slighted their opportunities.

Although Israel had "mocked the messengers of God, and despised His words, and misused His prophets" (2 Chronicles 36:16), He had still manifested Himself to them, as "the Lord God, merciful and gracious, long-suffering, and abundant in goodness and truth" (Exodus 34:6); notwithstanding repeated rejections, His mercy had continued its pleadings. With more than a father's pitying love for the son of his care, God had "sent to them by His messengers, rising up betimes, and sending; because He had compassion on His people, and on His dwelling place." 2 Chronicles 36:15. When remonstrance, entreaty, and rebuke had failed, He sent to them the best gift of heaven; nay, He poured out all heaven in that one Gift.

The Son of God Himself was sent to plead with the impenitent city. It was Christ that had brought Israel as a goodly vine out of Egypt. Psalm 80:8. His own hand had cast out the heathen before it. He had planted it "in a very fruitful hill." His guardian care had hedged it about. His servants had been sent to nurture it. "What could have been done more to My vineyard," He exclaims, "that I have not done in it?" Isaiah 5:1-4. Though when He looked that it should bring forth grapes, it brought forth wild grapes, yet with a still yearning hope of fruitfulness He came in person to His vineyard, if haply it might be saved from destruction. He digged about His vine; He pruned and cherished it. He was unwearied in His efforts to save this vine of His own planting.

For three years the Lord of light and glory had gone in and out among His people. He "went about doing good, and healing all that were oppressed of the devil," binding up the brokenhearted, setting at liberty them that were bound, restoring sight to the blind, causing the lame to walk and the deaf to hear, cleansing the lepers, raising the dead, and preaching the gospel to the poor. Acts 10:38; Luke 4:18; Matthew 11:5. To all classes alike was addressed the gracious call: "Come unto Me, all ye that labor and are heavy-laden, and I will give you rest." Matthew 11:28.

Though rewarded with evil for good, and hatred for His love (Psalm 109:5), He had steadfastly pursued His mission of mercy. Never were those repelled that sought His grace. A homeless wanderer, reproach and penury His daily lot, He lived to minister to the needs and lighten the woes of men, to plead with them to accept the gift of life. The waves of mercy, beaten back by those stubborn hearts, returned in a stronger tide of pitying, inexpressible love. But Israel had turned from her best Friend and only Helper. The pleadings of His love had been despised, His counsels spurned, His warnings ridiculed.

The hour of hope and pardon was fast passing; the cup of God's long-deferred wrath was almost full. The cloud that had been gathering through ages of apostasy and rebellion, now black with woe, was about to burst upon a guilty people; and He who alone could save them from their impending fate had been slighted, abused, rejected, and was soon to be crucified. When Christ should hang upon the cross of Calvary, Israel's day as a nation favored and blessed of God would be ended. The loss of even one soul is a calamity infinitely outweighing the gains and treasures of a world; but as Christ looked upon Jerusalem, the doom of a whole city, a whole nation, was before Him—that city, that nation, which had once been the chosen of God, His peculiar treasure.

Prophets had wept over the apostasy of Israel and the terrible desolations by which their sins were visited. Jeremiah wished that his eyes were a fountain of tears, that he might weep day and night for the slain of the daughter of his people, for the Lord's flock that was carried away captive. Jeremiah 9:1; 13:17. What, then, was the grief of Him whose prophetic glance took in, not years, but ages! He beheld the destroying angel with sword uplifted against the city which had so long been Jehovah's dwelling place. From the ridge of Olivet, the very spot afterward occupied by Titus and his army, He looked across the valley upon the sacred courts and porticoes, and with tear-dimmed eyes He saw, in awful perspective, the walls sur-rounded by alien hosts. He heard the tread of armies marshaling for war. He heard the voice of mothers and children crying for bread in the besieged city. He saw her holy and beautiful house, her palaces and towers, given to the flames, and where once they stood, only a heap of smoldering ruins.

Looking down the ages, He saw the covenant people scattered in every land, "like wrecks on a desert shore." In the temporal retribution about to fall upon her children, He saw but the first draft from that cup of wrath which at the final judgment she must drain to its dregs. Divine pity, yearning love, found utterance in the mournful words:

"O Jerusalem, Jerusalem, thou that killest the prophets, and stonest them which are sent unto thee, how often would I have gathered thy children together, even as a hen gathereth her chickens under her wings, and ye would not!" O that thou, a nation favored above every other, hadst known the time of thy visitation, and the things that belong unto thy peace! I have stayed the angel of justice, I have called thee to repentance, but in vain. It is not merely servants, delegates, and prophets, whom thou hast refused and rejected, but the Holy One of Israel, thy Redeemer. If thou art destroyed, thou alone art responsible. "Ye will not come to Me, that ye might have life." Matthew 23:37; John 5:40.

Christ saw in Jerusalem a symbol of the world hardened in unbelief and rebellion, and hastening on to meet the retributive judgments of God. The woes of a fallen race, pressing upon His soul, forced from His lips that exceeding bitter cry. He saw the record of sin traced in human misery, tears, and blood; His heart was moved with infinite pity for the afflicted and suffering ones of earth; He yearned to relieve them all. But even His hand might not turn back the tide of human woe; few would seek their only Source of help. He was willing to pour out His soul unto death, to bring salvation within their reach; but few would come to Him that they might have life.

The Majesty of heaven in tears! the Son of the infinite God troubled in spirit, bowed down with anguish! The scene filled all heaven with wonder. That scene reveals to us the exceeding sinfulness of sin; it shows how hard a task it is, even for Infinite Power, to save the guilty from the consequences of transgressing the law of God. Jesus, looking down to the last generation, saw the world involved in a deception similar to that which caused the destruction of Jerusalem. The great sin of the Jews was their rejection of Christ; the great sin of the Christian world would be their rejection of the law of God, the foundation of His government in heaven and earth. The precepts of Jehovah would be despised and set at nought. Millions in bondage to sin, slaves of Satan, doomed to suffer the second death, would refuse to listen to the words of truth in their day of visitation. Terrible blindness! strange infatuation!

Two days before the Passover, when Christ had for the last time departed from the temple, after denouncing the hypocrisy of the Jewish rulers, He again went out with His disciples to the Mount of Olives and seated Himself with them upon the grassy slope overlooking the city.

Once more He gazed upon its walls, its towers, and its palaces. Once more He beheld the temple in its dazzling splendor, a diadem of beauty crowning the sacred mount.

A thousand years before, the psalmist had magnified God's favor to Israel in making her holy house His dwelling place: "In Salem also is His tabernacle, and His dwelling place in Zion." He "chose the tribe of Judah, the Mount Zion which He loved. And He built His sanctuary like high palaces." Psalms 76:2; 78:68, 69. The first temple had been erected during the most prosperous period of Israel's history. Vast stores of treasure for this purpose had been collected by King David, and the plans for its construction were made by divine inspiration. 1 Chronicles 28:12, 19. Solomon, the wisest of Israel's monarchs, had completed the work. This temple was the most magnificent building which the world ever saw. Yet the Lord had declared by the prophet Haggai, concerning the second temple: "The glory of this latter house shall be greater than of the former." "I will shake all nations, and the Desire of all nations shall come: and I will fill this house with glory, saith the Lord of hosts." Haggai 2:9, 7.

After the destruction of the temple by Nebuchadnezzar it was rebuilt about five hundred years before the birth of Christ by a people who from a lifelong captivity had returned to a wasted and almost deserted country. There were then among them aged men who had seen the glory of Solomon's temple, and who wept at the foundation of the new building, that it must be so inferior to the former. The feeling that prevailed is forcibly described by the prophet: "Who is left among you that saw this house in her first glory? and how do ye see it now? is it not in your eyes in comparison of it as nothing?" Haggai 2:3; Ezra 3:12. Then was given the promise that the glory of this latter house should be greater than that of the former.

But the second temple had not equaled the first in magnificence; nor was it hallowed by those visible tokens of the divine presence which pertained to the first temple. There was no manifestation of supernatural power to mark its dedication. No cloud of glory was seen to fill the newly erected sanctuary. No fire from heaven descended to consume the sacrifice upon its altar. The Shekinah no longer abode between the cherubim in the most holy place; the ark, the mercy seat, and the tables of the testimony were not to be found therein. No voice sounded from heaven to make known to the inquiring priest the will of Jehovah.

For centuries the Jews had vainly endeavored to show wherein the promise of God given by Haggai had been fulfilled; yet pride and unbelief blinded their minds to the true meaning of the prophet's words. The second temple was not honored with the cloud of Jehovah's glory, but with the living presence of One in whom dwelt the fullness of the Godhead bodily—who was God Himself manifest in the flesh. The "Desire of all nations" had indeed come to His temple when the Man of Nazareth taught and healed in the sacred courts. In the presence of Christ, and in this only, did the second temple exceed the first in glory. But Israel had put from her the proffered Gift of heaven. With the humble Teacher who had that day passed out from its golden gate, the glory had forever departed from the temple. Already were the Saviour's words fulfilled: "Your house is left unto you desolate." Matthew 23:38.

The disciples had been filled with awe and wonder at Christ's prediction of the overthrow of the temple, and they desired to understand more fully the meaning of His words. Wealth, labor, and architectural skill had for more than forty years been freely expended to enhance its splendors. Herod the Great had lavished upon it both Roman wealth and Jewish treasure, and even the emperor of the world had enriched it with his gifts. Massive blocks of white marble, of almost fabulous size, forwarded from Rome for this purpose, formed a part of its structure; and to these the disciples had called the attention of their Master, saying: "See what manner of stones and what buildings are here!" Mark 13:1.

To these words, Jesus made the solemn and startling reply: "Verily I say unto you, There shall not be left here one stone upon another, that shall not be thrown down." Matthew 24:2.

With the overthrow of Jerusalem the disciples associated the events of Christ's personal coming in temporal glory to take the throne of universal empire, to punish the impenitent Jews, and to break from off the nation the Roman yoke. The Lord had told them that He would come the second time. Hence at the mention of judgments upon Jerusalem, their minds reverted to that coming; and as they were gathered about the Saviour upon the Mount of Olives, they asked: "When shall these things be? and what shall be the sign of Thy coming, and of the end of the world?" Verse 3.

The future was mercifully veiled from the disciples. Had they at that time fully comprehend the two awful facts—the Redeemer's sufferings and death, and the destruction of their city and temple—they would have been overwhelmed with horror. Christ presented before them an outline of the prominent events to take place before the close of time. His words were not then fully understood; but their meaning was to be unfolded as His people should need the instruction therein given. The prophecy which He uttered was twofold in its meaning; while foreshadowing the destruction of Jerusalem, it prefigured also the terrors of the last great day.

Jesus declared to the listening disciples the judgments that were to fall upon apostate Israel, and especially the retributive vengeance that would come upon them for their rejection and crucifixion of the Messiah. Unmistakable signs would precede the awful climax. The dreaded hour would come suddenly and swiftly. And the Saviour warned His followers: "When ye therefore shall see the abomination of desolation, spoken of by Daniel the prophet, stand in the holy place, (whoso readeth, let him understand:) then let them which be in Judea flee into the mountains." Matthew 24:15, 16; Luke 21:20, 21. When the idolatrous standards of the Romans should be set up in the holy ground, which extended some furlongs outside the city walls, then the followers of Christ were to find safety in flight. When the warning sign should be seen, those who would escape must make no delay. Throughout the land of Judea, as well as in Jerusalem itself, the signal for flight must be immediately obeyed. He who chanced to be upon the housetop must not go down into his house, even to save his most valued treasures. Those who were working in the fields or vineyards must not take time to return for the outer garment laid aside while they should be toiling in the heat of the day. They must not hesitate a moment, lest they be involved in the general destruction.

In the reign of Herod, Jerusalem had not only been greatly beautified, but by the erection of towers, walls, and fortresses, adding to the natural strength of its situation, it had been rendered apparently impregnable. He who would at this time have foretold publicly its destruction, would, like Noah in his day, have been called a crazed alarmist. But Christ had said: "Heaven and earth shall pass away, but My words shall not pass away." Matthew 24:35. Because of her sins, wrath had been denounced against Jerusalem, and her stubborn unbelief rendered her doom certain.

The Lord had declared by the prophet Micah: "Hear this, I pray you, ye heads of the house of Jacob, and princes of the house of Israel, that abhor judgment, and pervert all equity. They build up Zion with blood, and Jerusalem with iniquity. The heads thereof judge for reward, and the priests thereof teach for hire, and the prophets thereof divine for money: yet will they lean upon the Lord, and say, Is not the Lord among us? none evil can come upon us." Micah 3:9-11.

These words faithfully described the corrupt and self-righteous inhabitants of Jerusalem. While claiming to observe rigidly the precepts of God's law, they were transgressing all its principles. They hated Christ because His purity and holiness revealed their iniquity; and they accused Him of being the cause of all the troubles which had come upon them in consequence of their sins. Though they knew Him to be sinless, they had declared that His death was necessary to their safety as a nation. "If we let Him thus alone," said the Jewish leaders, "all men will believe on Him: and the Romans shall come and take away both our place and nation." John 11:48. If Christ were sacrificed, they might once more become a strong, united people. Thus they reasoned, and they concurred in the decision of their high priest, that it would be better for one man to die than for the whole nation to perish.

Thus the Jewish leaders had built up "Zion with blood, and Jerusalem with iniquity." Micah 3:10. And yet, while they slew their Saviour because He reproved their sins, such was their self-righteousness that they regarded themselves as God's favored people and expected the Lord to deliver them from their enemies. "Therefore," continued the prophet, "shall Zion for your sake be plowed as a field, and Jerusalem shall become heaps, and the mountain of the house as the high places of the forest." Verse 12.

For nearly forty years after the doom of Jerusalem had been pronounced by Christ Himself, the Lord delayed His judgments upon the city and the nation. Wonderful was the long-suffering of God toward the rejectors of His gospel and the murderers of His Son. The parable of the unfruitful tree represented God's dealings with the Jewish nation. The command had gone forth, "Cut it down; why cumbereth it the ground?" (Luke 13:7) but divine mercy had spared it yet a little longer. There were still many among the Jews who were ignorant of the character and the work of Christ. And the children had not enjoyed the opportunities or received the light which their parents had spurned. Through the preaching of the apostles and their associates, God would cause light to shine upon them; they would be permitted to see how prophecy had been fulfilled, not only in the birth and life of Christ, but in His death and resurrection. The children were not condemned for the sins of the parents; but when, with a knowledge of all the light given to their parents, the children rejected the additional light granted to themselves, they became partakers of the parents' sins, and filled up the measure of their iniquity.

The long-suffering of God toward Jerusalem only confirmed the Jews in their stubborn impenitence. In their hatred and cruelty toward the disciples of Jesus they rejected the last offer of mercy. Then God withdrew His protection from them and removed His restraining power from Satan and his angels, and the nation was left to the control of the leader she had chosen. Her children had spurned the grace of Christ, which would have enabled them to subdue their evil impulses, and now these became the conquerors. Satan aroused the fiercest and most debased passions of the soul. Men did not reason; they were beyond reason—controlled by impulse and blind rage. They became satanic in their cruelty. In the family and in the nation, among the highest and the lowest classes alike, there was suspicion, envy, hatred, strife, rebellion, murder. There was no safety anywhere. Friends and kindred betrayed one another. Parents slew their children, and children their parents. The rulers of the people had no power to rule themselves. Uncontrolled passions made them tyrants. The Jews had accepted false testimony to condemn the innocent Son of God. Now false accusations made their own lives uncertain. By their actions they had long been saying: "Cause the Holy One of Israel to cease from before us." Isaiah 30:11. Now their desire was granted. The fear of God no longer disturbed them. Satan was at the head of the nation, and the highest civil and religious authorities were under his sway.

The leaders of the opposing factions at times united to plunder and torture their wretched victims, and again they fell upon each other's forces and slaughtered without mercy. Even the sanctity of the temple could not restrain their horrible ferocity. The worshipers were stricken down before the altar, and the sanctuary was polluted with the bodies of the slain. Yet in their blind and blasphemous presumption the instigators of this hellish work publicly declared that they had no fear that Jerusalem would be destroyed, for it was God's own city. To establish their power more firmly, they bribed false prophets to proclaim, even while Roman legions were besieging the temple, that the people were to wait for deliverance from God. To the last, multitudes held fast to the belief that the Most High would interpose for the defeat of their adversaries. But Israel had spurned the divine protection, and now she had no defense. Unhappy Jerusalem! rent by internal dissensions, the blood of her children slain by one another's hands crimsoning her streets, while alien armies beat down her fortifications and slew her men of war!

All the predictions given by Christ concerning the destruction of Jerusalem were fulfilled to the letter. The Jews experienced the truth of His words of warning: "With what measure ye mete, it shall be measured to you again." Matthew 7:2.

Signs and wonders appeared, foreboding disaster and doom. In the midst of the night an unnatural light shone over the temple and the altar. Upon the clouds at sunset were pictured chariots and men of war gathering for battle. The priests ministering by night in the sanctuary were terrified by mysterious sounds; the earth trembled, and a multitude of voices were heard crying: "Let us depart hence." The great eastern gate, which was so heavy that it could hardly be shut by a score of men, and which was secured by immense bars of iron fastened deep in the pavement of solid stone, opened at midnight, without visible agency.—Milman, *The History of the Jews*, book 13.

For seven years a man continued to go up and down the streets of Jerusalem, declaring the woes that were to come upon the city. By day and by night he chanted the wild dirge: "A voice from the east! a voice from the west! a voice from the four winds! a voice against Jerusalem and against the temple! a voice against the bridegrooms and the brides! a voice against the whole people!"—*Ibid.* This strange being was imprisoned and scourged, but no complaint escaped his lips. To insult and abuse he answered only: "Woe, woe to Jerusalem!" "woe, woe to the inhabitants thereof!" His warning cry ceased not until he was slain in the siege he had foretold.

Not one Christian perished in the destruction of Jerusalem. Christ had given His disciples warning, and all who believed His words watched for the promised sign. "When ye shall see Jerusalem compassed with armies," said Jesus, "then know that the desolation thereof is nigh. Then let them which are in Judea flee to the mountains; and let them which are in the midst of it depart out." Luke 21:20, 21. After the Romans under Cestius had surrounded the city, they unexpectedly abandoned the siege when everything seemed favorable for an immediate attack. The besieged, despairing of successful resistance, were on the point of surrender, when the Roman general withdrew his forces without the least apparent reason. But God's merciful providence was directing events for the good of His own people. The promised sign had been given to the waiting Christians, and now an opportunity was offered for all who would, to obey the Saviour's warning. Events were so overruled that neither Jews nor Romans should hinder the flight of the Christians. Upon the retreat of Cestius, the Jews, sallying from Jerusalem, pursued after his retiring army; and while both forces were thus fully engaged, the Christians had an opportunity to leave the city. At this time the country also had been cleared of enemies who might have endeavored to intercept them. At the time of the siege, the Jews were assembled at Jerusalem to keep the Feast of Tabernacles, and thus the Christians throughout the land were able to make their escape unmolested. Without delay they fled to a place of safety—the city of Pella, in the land of Perea, beyond Jordan.

The Jewish forces, pursuing after Cestius and his army, fell upon their rear with such fierceness as to threaten them with total destruction. It was with great difficulty that the Romans succeeded in making their retreat. The Jews escaped almost without loss, and with their spoils returned in triumph to Jerusalem. Yet this apparent success brought them only evil. It inspired them with that spirit of stubborn resistance to the Romans which speedily brought unutterable woe upon the doomed city.

Terrible were the calamities that fell upon Jerusalem when the siege was resumed by Titus. The city was invested at the time of the Passover, when millions of Jews were assembled within its walls. Their stores of provision, which if carefully preserved would have supplied the inhabitants for years, had previously been destroyed through the jealousy and revenge of the contending factions, and now all the horrors of starvation were experienced. A measure of wheat was sold for a talent. So fierce were the pangs of hunger that men would gnaw the leather of their belts and sandals and the covering of their shields. Great numbers of the people would steal out at night to gather wild plants growing outside the city walls, though many were seized and put to death with cruel torture, and often those who returned in safety were robbed of what they had gleaned at so great peril. The most inhuman tortures were inflicted by those in power, to force from the want-stricken people the last scanty supplies which they might have concealed. And these cruelties were not infrequently practiced by men who were themselves well fed, and who were merely desirous of laying up a store of provision for the future.

Thousands perished from famine and pestilence. Natural affection seemed to have been destroyed. Husbands robbed their wives, and wives their husbands. Children would be seen snatching the food from the mouths of their aged parents. The question of the prophet, "Can a woman forget her sucking child?" received the answer within the walls of that doomed city: "The hands of the pitiful women have sodden their own children: they were their meat in the destruction of the daughter of my people." Isaiah 49:15; Lamentations 4:10. Again was fulfilled the warning prophecy given fourteen centuries before: "The tender and delicate woman among you, which would not adventure to set the sole of her foot upon the ground for delicateness and tenderness, her eye shall be evil toward the husband of her bosom, and toward her son, and toward her daughter, … and toward her children which she shall bear: for she shall eat them for want of all things secretly in the siege and straitness, wherewith thine enemy shall distress thee in thy gates." Deuteronomy 28:56, 57.

The Roman leaders endeavored to strike terror to the Jews and thus cause them to surrender. Those prisoners who resisted when taken, were scourged, tortured, and crucified before the wall of the city. Hundreds were daily put to death in this manner, and the dreadful work continued until, along the Valley of Jehoshaphat and at Calvary, crosses were erected in so great numbers that there was scarcely room to move among them. So terribly was visited that awful imprecation uttered before the judgment seat of Pilate: "His blood be on us, and on our children." Matthew 27:25.

Titus would willingly have put an end to the fearful scene, and thus have spared Jerusalem the full measure of her doom. He was filled with horror as he saw the bodies of the dead lying in heaps in the valleys. Like one entranced, he looked from the crest of Olivet upon the magnificent temple and gave command that not one stone of it be touched. Before attempting to gain possession of this stronghold, he made an earnest appeal to the Jewish leaders not to force him to defile the sacred place with blood. If they would come forth and fight in any other place, no Roman should violate the sanctity of the temple. Josephus himself, in a most eloquent appeal, entreated them to surrender, to save themselves, their city, and their place of worship. But his words were answered with bitter curses. Darts were hurled at him, their last human mediator, as he stood pleading with them. The Jews had rejected the entreaties of the Son of God, and now expostulation and entreaty only made them more determined to resist to the last. In vain were the efforts of Titus to save the temple; One greater than he had declared that not one stone was to be left upon another.

The blind obstinacy of the Jewish leaders, and the detestable crimes perpetrated within the besieged city, excited the horror and indignation of the Romans, and Titus at last decided to take the temple by storm. He determined, however, that if possible it should be saved from destruction. But his commands were disregarded. After he had retired to his tent at night, the Jews, sallying from the temple, attacked the soldiers without. In the struggle, a firebrand was flung by a soldier through an opening in the porch, and immediately the cedar-lined chambers about the holy house were in a blaze. Titus rushed to the place, followed by his generals and legionaries, and commanded the soldiers to quench the flames. His words were unheeded. In their fury the soldiers hurled blazing brands into the chambers adjoining the temple, and then with their swords they slaughtered in great numbers those who had found shelter there. Blood flowed down the temple steps like water. Thousands upon thousands of Jews perished. Above the sound of battle, voices were heard shouting: "Ichabod!"—the glory is departed.

"Titus found it impossible to check the rage of the soldiery; he entered with his officers, and surveyed the interior of the sacred edifice. The splendor filled them with wonder; and as the flames had not yet penetrated to the holy place, he made a last effort to save it, and springing forth, again exhorted the soldiers to stay the progress of the conflagration. The centurion Liberalis endeavored to force obedience with his staff of office; but even respect for the emperor gave way to the furious animosity against the Jews, to the fierce excitement of battle, and to the insatiable hope of plunder. The soldiers saw everything around them radiant with gold, which shone dazzlingly in the wild light of the flames; they supposed that incalculable treasures were laid up in the sanctuary. A soldier, unperceived, thrust a lighted torch between the hinges of the door: the whole building was in flames in an instant. The blinding smoke and fire forced the officers to retreat, and the noble edifice was left to its fate.

"It was an appalling spectacle to the Roman—what was it to the Jew? The whole summit of the hill which commanded the city, blazed like a volcano. One after another the buildings fell in, with a tremendous crash, and were swallowed up in the fiery abyss. The roofs of cedar were like sheets of flame; the gilded pinnacles shone like spikes of red light; the gate towers sent up tall columns of flame and smoke. The neighboring hills were lighted up; and dark groups of people were seen watching in horrible anxiety the progress of the destruction: the walls and heights of the upper city were crowded with faces, some pale with the agony of despair, others scowling unavailing vengeance. The shouts of the Roman soldiery as they ran to and fro, and the howlings of the insurgents who were perishing in the flames, mingled with the roaring of the conflagration and the thundering sound of falling timbers. The echoes of the mountains replied or brought back the shrieks of the people on the heights; all along the walls resounded screams and wailings; men who were expiring with famine rallied their remaining strength to utter a cry of anguish and desolation.

"The slaughter within was even more dreadful than the spectacle from without. Men and women, old and young, insurgents and priests, those who fought and those who entreated mercy, were hewn down in indiscriminate carnage. The number of the slain exceeded that of the slayers. The legionaries had to clamber over heaps of dead to carry on the work of extermination."—Milman, *The History of the Jews*, book 16.

After the destruction of the temple, the whole city soon fell into the hands of the Romans. The leaders of the Jews forsook their impregnable towers, and Titus found them solitary. He gazed upon them with amazement, and declared that God had given them into his hands; for no engines, however powerful, could have prevailed against those stupendous battlements. Both the city and the temple were razed to their foundations, and the ground upon which the holy house had stood was "plowed like a field." Jeremiah 26:18. In the siege and the slaughter that followed, more than a million of the people perished; the survivors were carried away as captives, sold as slaves, dragged to Rome to grace the conqueror's triumph, thrown to wild beasts in the amphitheaters, or scattered as homeless wanderers throughout the earth.

The Jews had forged their own fetters; they had filled for themselves the cup of vengeance. In the utter destruction that befell them as a nation, and in all the woes that followed them in their dispersion, they were but reaping the harvest which their own hands had sown. Says the prophet: "O Israel, thou hast destroyed thyself;" "for thou hast fallen by thine iniquity." Hosea 13:9; 14:1. Their sufferings are often represented as a punishment visited upon them by the direct decree of God. It is thus that the great deceiver seeks to conceal his own work. By stubborn rejection of divine love and mercy, the Jews had caused the protection of God to be withdrawn from them, and Satan was permitted to rule them according to his will. The horrible cruelties enacted in the destruction of Jerusalem are a demonstration of Satan's vindictive power over those who yield to his control.

We cannot know how much we owe to Christ for the peace and protection which we enjoy. It is the restraining power of God that prevents mankind from passing fully under the control of Satan. The disobedient and unthankful have great reason for gratitude for God's mercy and long-suffering in holding in check the cruel, malignant power of the evil one. But when men pass the limits of divine forbearance, that restraint is removed. God does not stand toward the sinner as an executioner of the sentence against transgression; but He leaves the rejectors of His mercy to themselves, to reap that which they have sown. Every ray of light rejected, every warning despised or unheeded, every passion indulged, every transgression of the law of God, is a seed sown which yields its unfailing harvest. The Spirit of God, persistently resisted, is at last withdrawn from the sinner, and then there is left no power to control the evil passions of the soul, and no protection from the malice and enmity of Satan. The destruction of Jerusalem is a fearful and solemn warning to all who are trifling with the offers of divine grace and resisting the pleadings of divine mercy. Never was there given a more decisive testimony to God's hatred of sin and to the certain punishment that will fall upon the guilty.

The Saviour's prophecy concerning the visitation of judgments upon Jerusalem is to have another fulfillment, of which that terrible desolation was but a faint shadow. In the fate of the chosen city we may behold the doom of a world that has rejected God's mercy and trampled upon His law. Dark are the records of human misery that earth has witnessed during its long centuries of crime. The heart sickens, and the mind grows faint in contemplation. Terrible have been the results of rejecting the authority of Heaven. But a scene yet darker is presented in the revelations of the future. The records of the past,—the long procession of tumults, conflicts, and revolutions, the "battle of the warrior ... with confused noise, and garments rolled in blood" (Isaiah 9:5),— what are these, in contrast with the terrors of that day when the restraining Spirit of God shall be wholly withdrawn from the wicked, no longer to hold in check the outburst of human passion and satanic wrath! The world will then behold, as never before, the results of Satan's rule.

But in that day, as in the time of Jerusalem's destruction, God's people will be delivered, everyone that shall be found written among the living. Isaiah 4:3. Christ has declared that He will come the second time to gather His faithful ones to Himself: "Then shall all the tribes of the earth mourn, and they shall see the Son of man coming in the clouds of heaven with power and great glory. And He shall send His angels with a great sound of a trumpet, and they shall gather together His elect from the four winds, from one end of heaven to the other." Matthew 24:30, 31. Then shall they that obey not the gospel be consumed with the spirit of His mouth and be destroyed with the brightness of His coming. 2 Thessalonians 2:8. Like Israel of old the wicked destroy themselves; they fall by their iniquity. By a life of sin, they have placed themselves so out of harmony with God, their natures have become so debased with evil, that the manifestation of His glory is to them a consuming fire.

Let men beware lest they neglect the lesson conveyed to them in the words of Christ. As He warned His disciples of Jerusalem's destruction, giving them a sign of the approaching ruin, that they might make their escape; so He has warned the world of the day of final destruction and has given them tokens of its approach, that all who will may flee from the wrath to come. Jesus declares: "There shall be signs in the sun, and in the moon, and in the stars; and upon the earth distress of nations." Luke 21:25; Matthew 24:29; Mark 13:24-26; Revelation 6:12-17. Those who behold these harbingers of His coming are to "know that it is near, even at the doors." Matthew 24:33. "Watch ye therefore," are His words of admonition. Mark 13:35. They that heed the warning shall not be left in darkness, that that day should overtake them unawares. But to them that will not watch, "the day of the Lord so cometh as a thief in the night." 1 Thessalonians 5:2-5.

The world is no more ready to credit the message for this time than were the Jews to receive the Saviour's warning concerning Jerusalem. Come when it may, the day of God will come unawares to the ungodly. When life is going on in its unvarying round; when men are absorbed in pleasure, in business, in traffic, in money-making; when religious leaders are magnifying the world's progress and enlightenment, and the people are lulled in a false security—then, as the midnight thief steals within the unguarded dwelling, so shall sudden destruction come upon the careless and ungodly, "and they shall not escape." Verse 3.

Two

—The Scriptures as a Safeguard—

"To the law and to the testimony: if they speak not according to this word, it is because there is no light in them." Isaiah 8:20. The people of God are directed to the Scriptures as their safeguard against the influence of false teachers and the delusive power of spirits of darkness. Satan employs every possible device to prevent men from obtaining a knowledge of the Bible; for its plain utterances reveal his deceptions. At every revival of God's work the prince of evil is aroused to more intense activity; he is now putting forth his utmost efforts for a final struggle against Christ and His followers. The last great delusion is soon to open before us. Antichrist is to perform his marvelous works in our sight. So closely will the counterfeit resemble the true that it will be impossible to distinguish between them except by the Holy Scriptures. By their testimony every statement and every miracle must be tested.

Those who endeavor to obey all the commandments of God will be opposed and derided. They can stand only in God. In order to endure the trial before them, they must understand the will of God as revealed in His word; they can honor Him only as they have a right conception of His character, government, and purposes, and act in accordance with them. None but those who have fortified the mind with the truths of the Bible will stand through the last great conflict. To every soul will come the searching test: Shall I obey God rather than men? The decisive hour is even now at hand. Are our feet planted on the rock of God's immutable word? Are we prepared to stand firm in defense of the commandments of God and the faith of Jesus?

Before His crucifixion the Saviour explained to His disciples that He was to be put to death and to rise again from the tomb, and angels were present to impress His words on minds and hearts. But the disciples were looking for temporal deliverance from the Roman yoke, and they could not tolerate the thought that He in whom all their hopes centered should suffer an ignominious death. The words which they needed to remember were banished from their minds; and when the time of trial came, it found them unprepared. The death of Jesus as fully destroyed their hopes as if He had not forewarned them. So in the prophecies the future is opened before us as plainly as it was opened to the disciples by the words of Christ. The events connected with the close of probation and the work of preparation for the time of trouble, are clearly presented. But multitudes have no more understanding of these important truths than if they had never been revealed. Satan watches to catch away every impression that would make them wise unto salvation, and the time of trouble will find them unready.

When God sends to men warnings so important that they are represented as proclaimed by holy angels flying in the midst of heaven, He requires every person endowed with reasoning powers to heed the message. The fearful judgments denounced against the worship of the beast and his image (Revelation 14:9-11), should lead all to a diligent study of the prophecies to learn what the mark of the beast is, and how they are to avoid receiving it. But the masses of the people turn away their ears from hearing the truth and are turned unto fables. The apostle Paul declared, looking down to the last days: "The time will come when they will not endure sound doctrine." 2 Timothy 4:3. That time has fully come. The multitudes do not want Bible truth, because it interferes with the desires of the sinful, world-loving heart; and Satan supplies the deceptions which they love.

But God will have a people upon the earth to maintain the Bible, and the Bible only, as the standard of all doctrines and the basis of all reforms. The opinions of learned men, the deductions of science, the creeds or decisions of ecclesiastical councils, as numerous and discordant as are the churches which they represent, the voice of the majority—not one nor all of these should be regarded as evidence for or against any point of religious faith. Before accepting any doctrine or precept, we should demand a plain "Thus saith the Lord" in its support.

Satan is constantly endeavoring to attract attention to man in the place of God. He leads the people to look to bishops, to pastors, to professors of theology, as their guides, instead of searching the Scriptures to learn their duty for themselves. Then, by controlling the minds of these leaders, he can influence the multitudes according to his will.

When Christ came to speak the words of life, the common people heard Him gladly; and many, even of the priests and rulers, believed on Him. But the chief of the priesthood and the leading men of the nation were determined to condemn and repudiate His teachings. Though they were baffled in all their efforts to find accusations against Him, though they could not but feel the influence of the divine power and wisdom attending His words, yet they incased themselves in prejudice; they rejected the clearest evidence of His Messiahship, lest they should be forced to become His disciples. These opponents of Jesus were men whom the people had been taught from infancy to reverence, to whose authority they had been accustomed implicitly to bow. "How is it," they asked, "that our rulers and learned scribes do not believe on Jesus? Would not these pious men receive Him if He were the Christ?" It was the influence of such teachers that led the Jewish nation to reject their Redeemer.

The spirit which actuated those priests and rulers is still manifested by many who make a high profession of piety. They refuse to examine the testimony of the Scriptures concerning the special truths for this time. They point to their own numbers, wealth, and popularity, and look with contempt upon the advocates of truth as few, poor, and unpopular, having a faith that separates them from the world.

Christ foresaw that the undue assumption of authority indulged by the scribes and Pharisees would not cease with the dispersion of the Jews. He had a prophetic view of the work of exalting human authority to rule the conscience, which has been so terrible a curse to the church in all ages. And His fearful denunciations of the scribes and Pharisees, and His warnings to the people not to follow these blind leaders, were placed on record as an admonition to future generations.

The Roman Church reserves to the clergy the right to interpret the Scriptures. On the ground that ecclesiastics alone are competent to explain God's word, it is withheld from the common people. Though the Reformation gave the Scriptures to all, yet the selfsame principle which was maintained by Rome prevents multitudes in Protestant churches from searching the Bible for themselves. They are taught to accept its teachings *as interpreted by the church*; and there are thousands who dare receive nothing, however plainly revealed in Scripture, that is contrary to their creed or the established teaching of their church.

Notwithstanding the Bible is full of warnings against false teachers, many are ready thus to commit the keeping of their souls to the clergy. There are today thousands of professors of religion who can give no other reason for points of faith which they hold than that they were so instructed by their religious leaders. They pass by the Saviour's teachings almost unnoticed, and place implicit confidence in the words of the ministers. But are ministers infallible? How can we trust our souls to their guidance unless we know from God's word that they are light bearers? A lack of moral courage to step aside from the beaten track of the world leads many to follow in the steps of learned men; and by their reluctance to investigate for themselves, they are becoming hopelessly fastened in the chains of error. They see that the truth for this time is plainly brought to view in the Bible; and they feel the power of the Holy Spirit attending its proclamation; yet they allow the opposition of the clergy to turn them from the light. Though reason and conscience are convinced, these deluded souls dare not think differently from the minister; and their individual judgment, their eternal interests, are sacrificed to the unbelief, the pride and prejudice, of another.

Many are the ways by which Satan works through human influence to bind his captives. He secures multitudes to himself by attaching them by the silken cords of affection to those who are enemies of the cross of Christ. Whatever this attachment may be, parental, filial, conjugal, or social, the effect is the same; the opposers of truth exert their power to control the conscience, and the souls held under their sway have not sufficient courage or independence to obey their own convictions of duty.

The truth and the glory of God are inseparable; it is impossible for us, with the Bible within our reach, to honor God by erroneous opinions. Many claim that it matters not what one believes, if his life is only right. But the life is molded by the faith. If light and truth is within our reach, and we neglect to improve the privilege of hearing and seeing it, we virtually reject it; we are choosing darkness rather than light.

"There is a way that seemeth right unto a man, but the end thereof are the ways of death." Proverbs 16:25. Ignorance is no excuse for error or sin, when there is every opportunity to know the will of God.

A man is traveling and comes to a place where there are several roads and a guideboard indicating where each one leads. If he disregards the guideboard, and takes whichever road seems to him to be right, he may be ever so sincere, but will in all probability find himself on the wrong road.

God has given us His word that we may become acquainted with its teachings and know for ourselves what He requires of us. When the lawyer came to Jesus with the inquiry, "What shall I do to inherit eternal life?" the Saviour referred him to the Scriptures, saying: "What is written in the law? how readest thou?" Ignorance will not excuse young or old, nor release them from the punishment due for the transgression of God's law; because there is in their hands a faithful presentation of that law and of its principles and claims. It is not enough to have good intentions; it is not enough to do what a man thinks is right or what the minister tells him is right. His soul's salvation is at stake, and he should search the Scriptures for himself. However strong may be his convictions, however confident he may be that the minister knows what is truth, this is not his foundation. He has a chart pointing out every waymark on the heavenward journey, and he ought not to guess at anything.

It is the first and highest duty of every rational being to learn from the Scriptures what is truth, and then to walk in the light and encourage others to follow his example. We should day by day study the Bible diligently, weighing every thought and comparing scripture with scripture. With divine help we are to form our opinions for ourselves as we are to answer for ourselves before God.

The truths most plainly revealed in the Bible have been involved in doubt and darkness by learned men, who, with a pretense of great wisdom, teach that the Scriptures have a mystical, a secret, spiritual meaning not apparent in the language employed. These men are false teachers. It was to such a class that Jesus declared: "Ye know not the Scriptures, neither the power of God." Mark 12:24. The language of the Bible should be explained according to its obvious meaning, unless a symbol or figure is employed. Christ has given the promise: "If any man will do His will, he shall know of the doctrine." John 7:17. If men would but take the Bible as it reads, if there were no false teachers to mislead and confuse their minds, a work would be accomplished that would make angels glad and that would bring into the fold of Christ thousands upon thousands who are now wandering in error.

We should exert all the powers of the mind in the study of the Scriptures and should task the understanding to comprehend, as far as mortals can, the deep things of God; yet we must not forget that the docility and submission of a child is the true spirit of the learner. Scriptural difficulties can never be mastered by the same methods that are employed in grappling with philosophical problems. We should not engage in the study of the Bible with that self-reliance with which so many enter the domains of science, but with a prayerful dependence upon God and a sincere desire to learn His will. We must come with a humble and teachable spirit to obtain knowledge from the great I AM. Otherwise, evil angels will so blind our minds and harden our hearts that we shall not be impressed by the truth.

Many a portion of Scripture which learned men pronounce a mystery, or pass over as unimportant, is full of comfort and instruction to him who has been taught in the school of Christ. One reason why many theologians have no clearer understanding of God's word is, they close their eyes to truths which they do not wish to practice. An understanding of Bible truth depends not so much on the power of intellect brought to the search as on the singleness of purpose, the earnest longing after righteousness.

The Bible should never be studied without prayer. The Holy Spirit alone can cause us to feel the importance of those things easy to be understood, or prevent us from wresting truths difficult of comprehension. It is the office of heavenly angels to prepare the heart so to comprehend God's word that we shall be charmed with its beauty, admonished by its warnings, or animated and strengthened by its promises. We should make the psalmist's petition our own: "Open Thou mine eyes, that I may behold wondrous things out of Thy law." Psalm 119:18. Temptations often appear irresistible because, through neglect of prayer and the study of the Bible, the tempted one cannot readily remember God's promises and meet Satan with the Scripture weapons. But angels are round about those who are willing to be taught in divine things; and in the time of great necessity they will bring to their remembrance the very truths which are needed. Thus "when the enemy shall come in like a flood, the Spirit of the Lord shall lift up a standard against him." Isaiah 59:19.

Jesus promised His disciples: "The Comforter, which is the Holy Ghost, whom the Father will send in My name, He shall teach you all things, and bring all things to your remembrance, whatsoever I have said unto you." John 14:26. But the teachings of Christ must previously have been stored in the mind in order for the Spirit of God to bring them to our remembrance in the time of peril. "Thy word have I hid in mine heart," said David, "that I might not sin against Thee." Psalm 119:11.

All who value their eternal interests should be on their guard against the inroads of skepticism. The very pillars of truth will be assailed. It is impossible to keep beyond the reach of the sarcasms and sophisms, the insidious and pestilent teachings, of modern infidelity. Satan adapts his temptations to all classes. He assails the illiterate with a jest or sneer, while he meets the educated with scientific objections and philosophical reasoning, alike calculated to excite distrust or contempt of the Scriptures. Even youth of little experience presume to insinuate doubts concerning the fundamental principles of Christianity. And this youthful infidelity, shallow as it is, has its influence. Many are thus led to jest at the faith of their fathers and to do despite to the Spirit of grace. Hebrews 10:29. Many a life that promised to be an honor to God and a blessing to the world has been blighted by the foul breath of infidelity. All who trust to the boastful decisions of human reason and imagine that they can explain divine mysteries and arrive at truth unaided by the wisdom of God are entangled in the snare of Satan.

We are living in the most solemn period of this world's history. The destiny of earth's teeming multitudes is about to be decided. Our own future well-being and also the salvation of other souls depend upon the course which we now pursue. We need to be guided by the Spirit of truth. Every follower of Christ should earnestly inquire: "Lord, what wilt Thou have me to do?" We need to humble ourselves before the Lord, with fasting and prayer, and to meditate much upon His word, especially upon the scenes of the judgment. We should now seek a deep and living experience in the things of God. We have not a moment to lose. Events of vital importance are taking place around us; we are on Satan's enchanted ground. Sleep not, sentinels of God; the foe is lurking near, ready at any moment, should you become lax and drowsy, to spring upon you and make you his prey.

Many are deceived as to their true condition before God. They congratulate themselves upon the wrong acts which they do not commit, and forget to enumerate the good and noble deeds which God requires of them, but which they have neglected to perform. It is not enough that they are trees in the garden of God. They are to answer His expectation by bearing fruit. He holds them accountable for their failure to accomplish all the good which they could have done, through His grace strengthening them. In the books of heaven they are registered as cumberers of the ground. Yet the case of even this class is not utterly hopeless. With those who have slighted God's mercy and abused His grace, the heart of long-suffering love yet pleads. "Wherefore He saith, Awake thou that sleepest, and arise from the dead, and Christ shall give thee light. See then that ye walk circumspectly, ... redeeming the time, because the days are evil." Ephesians 5:14-16.

When the testing time shall come, those who have made God's word their rule of life will be revealed. In summer there is no noticeable difference between evergreens and other trees; but when the blasts of winter come, the evergreens remain unchanged, while other trees are stripped of their foliage. So the falsehearted professor may not now be distinguished from the real Christian, but the time is just upon us when the difference will be apparent. Let opposition arise, let bigotry and intolerance again bear sway, let persecution be kindled, and the halfhearted and hypocritical will waver and yield the faith; but the true Christian will stand firm as a rock, his faith stronger, his hope brighter, than in days of prosperity.

Says the psalmist: "Thy testimonies are my meditation." "Through Thy precepts I get understanding: therefore I hate every false way." Psalm 119:99, 104.

"Happy is the man that findeth wisdom." "He shall be as a tree planted by the waters, and that spreadeth out her roots by the river, and shall not see when heat cometh, but her leaf shall be green; and shall not be careful in the year of drought, neither shall cease from yielding fruit." Proverbs 3:13; Jeremiah 17:8.

Three

—God's Law Immutable—

"The temple of God was opened in heaven, and there was seen in His temple the ark of His testament." Revelation 11:19. The ark of God's testament is in the holy of holies, the second apartment of the sanctuary. In the ministration of the earthly tabernacle, which served "unto the example and shadow of heavenly things," this apartment was opened only upon the great Day of Atonement for the cleansing of the sanctuary. Therefore the announcement that the temple of God was opened in heaven and the ark of His testament was seen points to the opening of the most holy place of the heavenly sanctuary in 1844 as Christ entered there to perform the closing work of the atonement. Those who by faith followed their great High Priest as He entered upon His ministry in the most holy place, beheld the ark of His testament. As they had studied the subject of the sanctuary they had come to understand the Saviour's change of ministration, and they saw that He was now officiating before the ark of God, pleading His blood in behalf of sinners.

The ark in the tabernacle on earth contained the two tables of stone, upon which were inscribed the precepts of the law of God. The ark was merely a receptacle for the tables of the law, and the presence of these divine precepts gave to it its value and sacredness. When the temple of God was opened in heaven, the ark of His testament was seen. Within the holy of holies, in the sanctuary in heaven, the divine law is sacredly enshrined—the law that was spoken by God Himself amid the thunders of Sinai and written with His own finger on the tables of stone.

The law of God in the sanctuary in heaven is the great original, of which the precepts inscribed upon the tables of stone and recorded by Moses in the Pentateuch were an unerring transcript. Those who arrived at an understanding of this important point were thus led to see the sacred, unchanging character of the divine law. They saw, as never before, the force of the Saviour's words: "Till heaven and earth pass, one jot or one tittle shall in no wise pass from the law." Matthew 5:18. The law of God, being a revelation of His will, a transcript of His character, must forever endure, "as a faithful witness in heaven." Not one command has been annulled; not a jot or tittle has been changed. Says the psalmist: "Forever, O Lord, Thy word is settled in heaven." "All His commandments are sure. They stand fast for ever and ever." Psalms 119:89; 111:7, 8.

In the very bosom of the Decalogue is the fourth commandment, as it was first proclaimed: "Remember the Sabbath day, to keep it holy. Six days shalt thou labor, and do all thy work: but the seventh day is the Sabbath of the Lord thy God: in it thou shalt not do any work, thou, nor thy son, nor thy daughter, thy manservant, nor thy maidservant, nor thy cattle, nor thy stranger that is within thy gates: for in six days the Lord made heaven and earth, the sea, and all that in them is, and rested the seventh day: wherefore the Lord blessed the Sabbath day, and hallowed it." Exodus 20:8-11.

The Spirit of God impressed the hearts of those students of His word. The conviction was urged upon them that they had ignorantly transgressed this precept by disregarding the Creator's rest day. They began to examine the reasons for observing the first day of the week instead of the day which God had sanctified. They could find no evidence in the Scriptures that the fourth commandment had been abolished, or that the Sabbath had been changed; the blessing which first hallowed the seventh day had never been removed. They had been honestly seeking to know and to do God's will; now, as they saw themselves transgressors of His law, sorrow filled their hearts, and they manifested their loyalty to God by keeping His Sabbath holy.

Many and earnest were the efforts made to overthrow their faith. None could fail to see that if the earthly sanctuary was a figure or pattern of the heavenly, the law deposited in the ark on earth was an exact transcript of the law in the ark in heaven; and that an acceptance of the truth concerning the heavenly sanctuary involved an acknowledgment of the claims of God's law and the obligation of the Sabbath of the fourth commandment. Here was the secret of the bitter and determined opposition to the harmonious exposition of the Scriptures that revealed the ministration of Christ in the heavenly sanctuary. Men sought to close the door which God had opened, and to open the door which He had closed. But "He that openeth, and no man shutteth; and shutteth, and no man openeth," had declared: "Behold, I have set before thee an open door, and no man can shut it." Revelation 3:7, 8. Christ had opened the door, or ministration, of the most holy place, light was shining from that open door of the sanctuary in heaven, and the fourth commandment was shown to be included in the law which is there enshrined; what God had established, no man could overthrow.

Those who had accepted the light concerning the mediation of Christ and the perpetuity of the law of God found that these were the truths presented in Revelation 14. The messages of this chapter constitute a threefold warning which is to prepare the inhabitants of the earth for the Lord's second coming. The announcement, "The hour of His judgment is come," points to the closing work of Christ's ministration for the salvation of men. It heralds a truth which must be proclaimed until the Saviour's intercession shall cease and He shall return to the earth to take His people to Himself. The work of judgment which began in 1844 must continue until the cases of all are decided, both of the living and the dead; hence it will extend to the close of human probation. That men may be prepared to stand in the judgment, the message commands them to "fear God, and give glory to Him," "and worship Him that made heaven, and earth, and the sea, and the fountains of waters." The result of an acceptance of these messages is given in the word: "Here are they that keep the commandments of God, and the faith of Jesus." In order to be prepared for the judgment, it is necessary that men should keep the law of God. That law will be the standard of character in the judgment. The apostle Paul declares: "As many as have sinned in the law shall be judged by the law, ... in the day when God shall judge the secrets of men by Jesus Christ." And he says that "the doers of the law shall be justified." Romans 2:12-16. Faith is essential in order to the keeping of the law of God; for "without faith it is impossible to please Him." And "whatsoever is not of faith is sin." Hebrews 11:6; Romans 14:23.

By the first angel, men are called upon to "fear God, and give glory to Him" and to worship Him as the Creator of the heavens and the earth. In order to do this, they must obey His law. Says the wise man: "Fear God, and keep His commandments: for this is the whole duty of man." Ecclesiastes 12:13. Without obedience to His commandments no worship can be pleasing to God. "This is the love of God, that we keep His commandments." "He that turneth away his ear from hearing the law, even his prayer shall be abomination." 1 John 5:3; Proverbs 28:9.

The duty to worship God is based upon the fact that He is the Creator and that to Him all other beings owe their existence. And wherever, in the Bible, His claim to reverence and worship, above the gods of the heathen, is presented, there is cited the evidence of His creative power. "All the gods of the nations are idols: but the Lord made the heavens." Psalm 96:5. "To whom then will ye liken Me, or shall I be equal? saith the Holy One. Lift up your eyes on high, and behold who hath created these things." "Thus saith the Lord that created the heavens; God Himself that formed the earth and made it: ... I am the Lord; and there is none else." Isaiah 40:25, 26; 45:18. Says the psalmist: "Know ye that the Lord He is God: it is He that hath made us, and not we ourselves." "O come, let us worship and bow down: let us kneel before the Lord our Maker." Psalms 100:3; 95:6. And the holy beings who worship God in heaven state, as the reason why their homage is due to Him: "Thou art worthy, O Lord, to receive glory and honor and power: for Thou hast created all things." Revelation 4:11.

In Revelation 14, men are called upon to worship the Creator; and the prophecy brings to view a class that, as the result of the threefold message, are keeping the commandments of God. One of these commandments points directly to God as the Creator. The fourth precept declares: "The seventh day is the Sabbath of the Lord thy God: ... for in six days the Lord made heaven and earth, the sea, and all that in them is, and rested the seventh day: wherefore the Lord blessed the Sabbath day, and hallowed it." Exodus 20:10, 11. Concerning the Sabbath, the Lord says, further, that it is "a sign, ... that ye may know that I am the Lord your God." Ezekiel 20:20. And the reason given is: "For in six days the Lord made heaven and earth, and on the seventh day He rested, and was refreshed." Exodus 31:17.

"The importance of the Sabbath as the memorial of creation is that it keeps ever present the true reason why worship is due to God"—because He is the Creator, and we are His creatures. "The Sabbath therefore lies at the very foundation of divine worship, for it teaches this great truth in the most impressive manner, and no other institution does this. The true ground of divine worship, not of that on the seventh day merely, but of all worship, is found in the distinction between the Creator and

His creatures. This great fact can never become obsolete, and must never be forgotten."—J. N. Andrews, *History of the Sabbath*, chapter 27. It was to keep this truth ever before the minds of men, that God instituted the Sabbath in Eden; and so long as the fact that He is our Creator continues to be a reason why we should worship Him, so long the Sabbath will continue as its sign and memorial. Had the Sabbath been universally kept, man's thoughts and affections would have been led to the Creator as the object of reverence and worship, and there would never have been an idolater, an atheist, or an infidel. The keeping of the Sabbath is a sign of loyalty to the true God, "Him that made heaven, and earth, and the sea, and the fountains of waters." It follows that the message which commands men to worship God and keep His commandments will especially call upon them to keep the fourth commandment.

In contrast to those who keep the commandments of God and have the faith of Jesus, the third angel points to another class, against whose errors a solemn and fearful warning is uttered: "If any man worship the beast and his image, and receive his mark in his forehead, or in his hand, the same shall drink of the wine of the wrath of God." Revelation 14:9, 10. A correct interpretation of the symbols employed is necessary to an understanding of this message. What is represented by the beast, the image, the mark?

The line of prophecy in which these symbols are found begins with Revelation 12, with the dragon that sought to destroy Christ at His birth. The dragon is said to be Satan (Revelation 12:9); he it was that moved upon Herod to put the Saviour to death. But the chief agent of Satan in making war upon Christ and His people during the first centuries of the Christian Era was the Roman Empire, in which paganism was the prevailing religion. Thus while the dragon, primarily, represents Satan, it is, in a secondary sense, a symbol of pagan Rome.

In chapter 13 (verses 1-10) is described another beast, "like unto a leopard," to which the dragon gave "his power, and his seat, and great authority." This symbol, as most Protestants have believed, represents the papacy, which succeeded to the power and seat and authority once held by the ancient Roman empire. Of the leopardlike beast it is declared: "There was given unto him a mouth speaking great things and blasphemies. ... And he opened his mouth in blasphemy against God, to blaspheme His name, and His tabernacle, and them that dwell in heaven. And it was given unto him to make war with the saints, and to overcome them: and power was given him over all kindreds, and tongues, and nations." This prophecy, which is nearly identical with the description of the little horn of Daniel 7, unquestionably points to the papacy.

"Power was given unto him to continue forty and two months." And, says the prophet, "I saw one of his heads as it were wounded to death." And again: "He that leadeth into captivity shall go into captivity: he that killeth with the sword must be killed with the sword." The forty and two months are the same as the "time and times and the dividing of time," three years and a half, or 1,260 days, of Daniel 7—the time during which the papal power was to oppress God's people. This period, as stated in preceding chapters, began with the supremacy of the papacy, A.D. 538, and terminated in 1798. At that time the pope was made captive by the French army, the papal power received its deadly wound, and the prediction was fulfilled, "He that leadeth into captivity shall go into captivity."

At this point another symbol is introduced. Says the prophet: "I beheld another beast coming up out of the earth; and he had two horns like a lamb." Verse 11. Both the appearance of this beast and the manner of its rise indicate that the nation which it represents is unlike those presented under the preceding symbols. The great kingdoms that have ruled the world were presented to the prophet Daniel as beasts of prey, rising when "the four winds of the heaven strove upon the great sea." Daniel 7:2. In Revelation 17 an angel explained that waters represent "peoples, and multitudes, and nations, and tongues." Revelation 17:15. Winds are a symbol of strife. The four winds of heaven striving upon the great sea represent the terrible scenes of conquest and revolution by which kingdoms have attained to power.

But the beast with lamblike horns was seen "coming up out of the earth." Instead of overthrowing other powers to establish itself, the nation thus represented must arise in territory previously unoccupied and grow up gradually and peacefully. It could not, then, arise among the crowded and struggling nationalities of the Old World—that turbulent sea of "peoples, and multitudes, and nations, and tongues." It must be sought in the Western Continent.

What nation of the New World was in 1798 rising into power, giving promise of strength and greatness, and attracting the attention of the world? The application of the symbol admits of no question. One nation, and only one, meets the specifications of this prophecy; it points unmistakably to the United States of America. Again and again the thought, almost the exact words, of the sacred writer has been unconsciously employed by the orator and the historian in describing the rise and growth of this nation. The beast was seen "coming up out of the earth;" and, according to the translators, the word here rendered "coming up" literally signifies "to grow or spring up as a plant." And, as we have seen, the nation must arise in territory previously unoccupied. A prominent writer, describing the rise of the United States, speaks of "*the mystery of her coming forth from vacancy*," and says: "Like a *silent seed* we grew into empire."—G.A. Townsend, *The New World Compared With the Old*, page 462. A European journal in 1850 spoke of the United States as a wonderful empire, which was "emerging," and "*amid the silence of the earth* daily adding to its power and pride."—The *Dublin Nation*. Edward Everett, in an oration on the Pilgrim founders of this nation, said: "Did they look for a retired spot, inoffensive for its obscurity, and safe in its remoteness, where the little church of Leyden might enjoy the freedom of conscience? Behold the *mighty regions* over which, in *peaceful conquest*, ... they have borne the banners of the cross!"—Speech delivered at Plymouth, Massachusetts, Dec. 22, 1824, page 11.

"And he had two horns like a lamb." The lamblike horns indicate youth, innocence, and gentleness, fitly representing the character of the United States when presented to the prophet as "coming up" in 1798. Among the Christian exiles who first fled to America and sought an asylum from royal oppression and priestly intolerance were many who determined to establish a government upon the broad foundation of civil and religious liberty. Their views found place in the Declaration of Independence, which sets forth the great truth that "all men are created equal" and endowed with the inalienable right to "life, liberty, and the pursuit of happiness." And the Constitution guarantees to the people the right of self-government, providing that representatives elected by the popular vote shall enact and administer the laws. Freedom of religious faith was also granted, every man being permitted to worship God according to the dictates of his conscience. Republicanism and Protestantism became the fundamental principles of the nation. These principles are the secret of its power and prosperity. The oppressed and downtrodden throughout Christendom have turned to this land with interest and hope. Millions have sought its shores, and the United States has risen to a place among the most powerful nations of the earth.

But the beast with lamblike horns "spake as a dragon. And he exerciseth all the power of the first beast before him, and causeth the earth and them which dwell therein to worship the first beast, whose deadly wound was healed; ... saying to them that dwell on the earth, that they should make an image to the beast, which had the wound by a sword, and did live." Revelation 13:11-14.

The lamblike horns and dragon voice of the symbol point to a striking contradiction between the professions and the practice of the nation thus represented. The "speaking" of the nation is the action of its legislative and judicial authorities. By such action it will give the lie to those liberal and peaceful principles which it has put forth as the foundation of its policy. The prediction that it will speak "as a dragon" and exercise "all the power of the first beast" plainly foretells a development of the spirit of intolerance and persecution that was manifested by the nations represented by the dragon and the leopardlike beast. And the statement that the beast with two horns "causeth the earth and them which dwell therein to worship the first beast" indicates that the authority of this nation is to be exercised in enforcing some observance which shall be an act of homage to the papacy.

Such action would be directly contrary to the principles of this government, to the genius of its free institutions, to the direct and solemn avowals of the Declaration of Independence, and to the Constitution. The founders of the nation wisely sought to guard against the employment of secular power on the part of the church, with its inevitable result—intolerance and persecution. The Constitution provides that "Congress shall make no law respecting an establishment of religion, or prohibiting the free exercise thereof," and that "no religious test shall ever be required as a qualification to any office of public trust under the United States." Only in flagrant violation of these safeguards to the nation's liberty, can any religious observance be enforced by civil authority. But the inconsistency of such action is no greater than is represented in the symbol. It is the beast with lamblike horns—in profession pure, gentle, and harmless—that speaks as a dragon.

"Saying to them that dwell on the earth, that *they* should make an image to the beast." Here is clearly presented a form of government in which the legislative power rests with the people, a most striking evidence that the United States is the nation denoted in the prophecy.

But what is the "image to the beast"? and how is it to be formed? The image is made by the two-horned beast, and is an image *to* the beast. It is also called an image *of* the beast. Then to learn what the image is like and how it is to be formed we must study the characteristics of the beast itself—the papacy.

When the early church became corrupted by departing from the simplicity of the gospel and accepting heathen rites and customs, she lost the Spirit and power of God; and in order to control the consciences of the people, she sought the support of the secular power. The result was the papacy, a church that controlled the power of the state and employed it to further her own ends, especially for the punishment of "heresy." In order for the United States to form an image of the beast, the religious power must so control the civil government that the authority of the state will also be employed by the church to accomplish her own ends.

Whenever the church has obtained secular power, she has employed it to punish dissent from her doctrines. Protestant churches that have followed in the steps of Rome by forming alliance with worldly powers have manifested a similar desire to restrict liberty of conscience. An example of this is given in the long-continued persecution of dissenters by the Church of England. During the sixteenth and seventeenth centuries, thousands of nonconformist ministers were forced to flee from their churches, and many, both of pastors and people, were subjected to fine, imprisonment, torture, and martyrdom.

It was apostasy that led the early church to seek the aid of the civil government, and this prepared the way for the development of the papacy—the beast. Said Paul: "There" shall "come a falling away, … and that man of sin be revealed." 2 Thessalonians 2:3. So apostasy in the church will prepare the way for the image to the beast.

The Bible declares that before the coming of the Lord there will exist a state of religious declension similar to that in the first centuries. "In the last days perilous times shall come. For men shall be *lovers of their own selves*, covetous, boasters, proud, blasphemers, disobedient to parents, unthankful, unholy, without natural affection, trucebreakers, false accusers, incontinent, fierce, *despisers of those that are good*, traitors, heady, high-minded, *lovers of pleasures more than lovers of God; having a form of godliness*, but denying the power thereof." 2 Timothy 3:1-5. "Now the Spirit speaketh expressly, that in the latter times some shall depart from the faith, giving heed to seducing spirits, and doctrines of devils." 1 Timothy 4:1. Satan will work "with all power and signs and lying wonders, and with all deceivableness of unrighteousness." And all that "received not the love of the truth, that they might be saved," will be left to accept "strong delusion, that they should believe a lie." 2 Thessalonians 2:9-11. When this state of ungodliness shall be reached, the same results will follow as in the first centuries.

The wide diversity of belief in the Protestant churches is regarded by many as decisive proof that no effort to secure a forced uniformity can ever be made. But there has been for years, in churches of the Protestant faith, a strong and growing sentiment in favor of a union based upon common points of doctrine. To secure such a union, the discussion of subjects upon which all were not agreed—however important they might be from a Bible standpoint—must necessarily be waived.

Charles Beecher, in a sermon in the year 1846, declared that the ministry of "the evangelical Protestant denominations" is "not only formed all the way up under a tremendous pressure of merely human fear, but they live, and move, and breathe in a state of things radically corrupt, and appealing every hour to every baser element of their nature to hush up the truth, and bow the knee to the power of apostasy. Was not this the way things went with Rome? Are we not living her life over again? And what do we see just ahead? Another general council! A world's convention! Evangelical alliance, and universal creed!"—Sermon on "The Bible a Sufficient Creed," delivered at Fort Wayne, Indiana, Feb. 22, 1846. When this shall be gained, then, in the effort to secure complete uniformity, it will be only a step to the resort to force.

When the leading churches of the United States, uniting upon such points of doctrine as are held by them in common, shall influence the state to enforce their decrees and to sustain their institutions, then Protestant America will have formed an image of the Roman hierarchy, and the infliction of civil penalties upon dissenters will inevitably result.

The beast with two horns "causeth [commands] all, both small and great, rich and poor, free and bond, to receive a mark in their right hand, or in their foreheads: and that no man might buy or sell, save he that had the mark, or the name of the beast, or the number of his name." Revelation 13:16, 17. The third angel's warning is: "If any man worship the beast and his image, and receive his mark in his forehead, or in his hand, the same shall drink of the wine of the wrath of God." "The beast" mentioned in this message, whose worship is enforced by the two-horned beast, is the first, or leopardlike beast of Revelation 13—the papacy. The "image to the beast" represents that form of apostate Protestantism which will be developed when the Protestant churches shall seek the aid of the civil power for the enforcement of their dogmas. The "mark of the beast" still remains to be defined.

After the warning against the worship of the beast and his image the prophecy declares: "Here are they that keep the commandments of God, and the faith of Jesus." Since those who keep God's commandments are thus placed in contrast with those that worship the beast and his image and receive his mark, it follows that the keeping of God's law, on the one hand, and its violation, on the other, will make the distinction between the worshipers of God and the worshipers of the beast.

The special characteristic of the beast, and therefore of his image, is the breaking of God's commandments. Says Daniel, of the little horn, the papacy: "He shall think to change times and the law." Daniel 7:25, R.V. And Paul styled the same power the "man of sin," who was to exalt himself above God. One prophecy is a complement of the other. Only by changing God's law could the papacy exalt itself above God; whoever should understandingly keep the law as thus changed would be giving supreme honor to that power by which the change was made. Such an act of obedience to papal laws would be a mark of allegiance to the pope in the place of God.

The papacy has attempted to change the law of God. The second commandment, forbidding image worship, has been dropped from the law, and the fourth commandment has been so changed as to authorize the observance of the first instead of the seventh day as the Sabbath. But papists urge, as a reason for omitting the second commandment, that it is unnecessary, being included in the first, and that they are giving the law exactly as God designed it to be understood. This cannot be the change foretold by the prophet. An intentional, deliberate change is presented: "He shall *think* to change the times and the law." The change in the fourth commandment exactly fulfills the prophecy. For this the only authority claimed is that of the church. Here the papal power openly sets itself above God.

While the worshipers of God will be especially distinguished by their regard for the fourth commandment,—since this is the sign of His creative power and the witness to His claim upon man's reverence and homage,—the worshipers of the beast will be distinguished by their efforts to tear down the Creator's memorial, to exalt the institution of Rome. It was in behalf of the Sunday that popery first asserted its arrogant claims; and its first resort to the power of the state was to compel the observance of Sunday as "the Lord's day." But the Bible points to the seventh day, and not to the first, as the Lord's day. Said Christ: "The Son of man is Lord also of the Sabbath." The fourth commandment declares: "The seventh day is the Sabbath of the Lord." And by the prophet Isaiah the Lord designates it: "My holy day." Mark 2:28; Isaiah 58:13.

The claim so often put forth that Christ changed the Sabbath is disproved by His own words. In His Sermon on the Mount He said: "Think not that I am come to destroy the law, or the prophets: I am not come to destroy, but to fulfill. For verily I say unto you, Till heaven and earth pass, one jot or one tittle shall in no wise pass from the law, till all be fulfilled. Whosoever therefore shall break one of these least commandments, and shall teach men so, he shall be called the least in the kingdom of heaven: but whosoever shall do and teach them, the same shall be called great in the kingdom of heaven," Matthew 5:17-19.

It is a fact generally admitted by Protestants that the Scriptures give no authority for the change of the Sabbath. This is plainly stated in publications issued by the American Tract Society and the American Sunday School Union. One of these works acknowledges "the complete silence of the New Testament so far as any explicit command for the Sabbath [Sunday, the first day of the week] or definite rules for its observance are concerned."—George Elliott, *The Abiding Sabbath*, page 184.

Another says: "Up to the time of Christ's death, no change had been made in the day;" and, "so far as the record shows, they [the apostles] did not ... give any explicit command enjoining the abandonment of the seventh-day Sabbath, and its observance on the first day of the week."—A. E. Waffle, *The Lord's Day*, pages 186-188.

Roman Catholics acknowledge that the change of the Sabbath was made by their church, and declare that Protestants by observing Sunday are recognizing her power. In the *Catholic Catechism an Religion*, in answer to a question as to the day to be observed in obedience to the fourth commandment, this statement is made: "During the old law, Saturday was the day sanctified; but *the church*, instructed by Jesus Christ, and directed by the Spirit of God, has substituted Sunday for Saturday; so now we sanctify the first, not the seventh day. Sunday means, and now is, the day of the Lord."

As the sign of the authority of the Catholic Church, papist writers cite "the very act of changing the Sabbath into Sunday, which Protestants allow of; ... because by keeping Sunday, they acknowledge the church's power to ordain feasts, and to command them under sin."—Henry Tuberville, *An Abridgment of the Christian Doctrine*, page 58. What then is the change of the Sabbath, but the sign, or mark, of the authority of the Roman Church—"the mark of the beast"?

The Roman Church has not relinquished her claim to supremacy; and when the world and the Protestant churches accept a sabbath of her creating, while they reject the Bible Sabbath, they virtually admit this assumption. They may claim the authority of tradition and of the Fathers for the change; but in so doing they ignore the very principle which separates them from Rome—that "the Bible, and the Bible only, is the religion of Protestants." The papist can see that they are deceiving themselves, willingly closing their eyes to the facts in the case. As the movement for Sunday enforcement gains favor, he rejoices, feeling assured that it will eventually bring the whole Protestant world under the banner of Rome.

Romanists declare that "the observance of Sunday by the Protestants is an homage they pay, in spite of themselves, to the authority of the [Catholic] Church."—Mgr. Segur, *Plain Talk About the Protestantism of Today*, page 213. The enforcement of Sundaykeeping on the part of Protestant churches is an enforcement of the worship of the papacy—of the beast. Those who, understanding the claims of the fourth commandment, choose to observe the false instead of the true Sabbath are thereby paying homage to that power by which alone it is commanded. But in the very act of enforcing a religious duty by secular power, the churches would themselves form an image to the beast; hence the enforcement of Sundaykeeping in the United States would be an enforcement of the worship of the beast and his image.

But Christians of past generations observed the Sunday, supposing that in so doing they were keeping the Bible Sabbath; and there are now true Christians in every church, not excepting the Roman Catholic communion, who honestly believe that Sunday is the Sabbath of divine appointment. God accepts their sincerity of purpose and their integrity before Him. But when Sunday observance shall be enforced by law, and the world shall be enlightened concerning the obligation of the true Sabbath, then whoever shall transgress the command of God, to obey a precept which has no higher authority than that of Rome, will thereby honor popery above God. He is paying homage to Rome and to the power which enforces the institution ordained by Rome. He is worshipping the beast and his image. As men then reject the institution which God has declared to be the sign of His authority, and honor in its stead that which Rome has chosen as the token of her supremacy, they will thereby accept the sign of allegiance to Rome—"the mark of the beast." And it is not until the issue is thus plainly set before the people, and they are brought to choose between the commandments of God and the commandments of men, that those who continue in transgression will receive "the mark of the beast."

The most fearful threatening ever addressed to mortals is contained in the third angel's message. That must be a terrible sin which calls down the wrath of God unmingled with mercy. Men are not to be left in darkness concerning this important matter; the warning against this sin is to be given to the world before the visitation of God's judgments, that all may know why they are to be inflicted, and have opportunity to escape them. Prophecy declares that the first angel would make his announcement to "every nation, and kindred, and tongue, and people." The warning of the third angel, which forms a part of the same threefold message, is to be no less widespread. It is represented in the prophecy as being proclaimed with a loud voice, by an angel flying in the midst of heaven; and it will command the attention of the world.

In the issue of the contest all Christendom will be divided into two great classes—those who keep the commandments of God and the faith of Jesus, and those who worship the beast and his image and receive his mark. Although church and state will unite their power to compel "all, both small and great, rich and poor, free and bond" (Revelation 13:16), to receive "the mark of the beast," yet the people of God will not receive The prophet of Patmos beholds "them that had gotten the victory over ˙st, and over his image, and over his mark, and over the number ˙, stand on the sea of glass, having the harps of God" and g of Moses and the Lamb. Revelation 15:2, 3.

Four

—A Work of Reform—

"The work of Sabbath reform to be accomplished in the last days is foretold in the prophecy of Isaiah: "Thus saith the Lord, Keep ye judgment, and do justice: for My salvation is near to come, and My righteousness to be revealed. Blessed is the man that doeth this, and the son of man that layeth hold on it; that keepeth the Sabbath from polluting it, and keepeth his hand from doing any evil." "The sons of the stranger, that join themselves to the Lord, to serve Him, and to love the name of the Lord, to be His servants, everyone that keepeth the Sabbath from polluting it, and taketh hold of My covenant; even them will I bring to My holy mountain, and make them joyful in My house of prayer." Isaiah 56:1, 2, 6, 7.

These words apply in the Christian age, as shown by the context: "The Lord God which gathereth the outcasts of Israel saith, Yet will I gather others to him, beside those that are gathered unto him." Verse 8. Here is foreshadowed the gathering in of the Gentiles by the gospel. And upon those who then honor the Sabbath, a blessing is pronounced. Thus the obligation of the fourth commandment extends past the crucifixion, resurrection, and ascension of Christ, to the time when His servants should preach to all nations the message of glad tidings.

The Lord commands by the same prophet: "Bind up the testimony, seal the law among My disciples." Isaiah 8:16. The seal of God's law is found in the fourth commandment. This only, of all the ten, brings to view both the name and the title of the Lawgiver. It declares Him to be the Creator of the heavens and the earth, and thus shows His claim to reverence and worship above all others. Aside from this precept, there is nothing in the Decalogue to show by whose authority the law is given. When the Sabbath was changed by the papal power, the seal was taken from the law. The disciples of Jesus are called upon to restore it by exalting the Sabbath of the fourth commandment to its rightful position as the Creator's memorial and the sign of His authority.

"To the law and to the testimony." While conflicting doctrines and theories abound, the law of God is the one unerring rule by which all opinions, doctrines, and theories are to be tested. Says the prophet: "If they speak not according to this word, it is because there is no light in them." Verse 20.

Again, the command is given: "Cry aloud, spare not, lift up thy voice like a trumpet, and show My people their transgression, and the house of Jacob their sins." It is not the wicked world, but those whom the Lord designates as "my people," that are to be reproved for their transgressions. He declares further: "Yet they seek Me daily, and delight to know My ways, as a nation that did righteousness, and forsook not the ordinance of their God." Isaiah 58:1, 2. Here is brought to view a class who think themselves righteous and appear to manifest great interest in the service of God; but the stern and solemn rebuke of the Searcher of hearts proves them to be trampling upon the divine precepts.

The prophet thus points out the ordinance which has been forsaken: "Thou shalt raise up the foundations of many generations; and thou shalt be called, The repairer of the breach, The restorer of paths to dwell in. If thou turn away thy foot from the Sabbath, from doing thy pleasure on My holy day; and call the Sabbath a delight, the holy of the Lord, honorable; and shalt honor Him, not doing thine own ways, nor finding thine own pleasure, nor speaking thine own words: then shalt thou delight thyself in the Lord." Verses 12-14. This prophecy also applies in our time. The breach was made in the law of God when the Sabbath was changed by the Roman power. But the time has come for that divine institution to be restored. The breach is to be repaired and the foundation of many generations to be raised up.

Hallowed by the Creator's rest and blessing, the Sabbath was kept by Adam in his innocence in holy Eden; by Adam, fallen yet repentant, when he was driven from his happy estate. It was kept by all the patriarchs, from Abel to righteous Noah, to Abraham, to Jacob. When the chosen people were in bondage in Egypt, many, in the midst of prevailing idolatry, lost their knowledge of God's law; but when the Lord delivered Israel, He proclaimed His law in awful grandeur to the assembled multitude, that they might know His will and fear and obey Him forever.

From that day to the present the knowledge of God's law has been preserved in the earth, and the Sabbath of the fourth commandment has been kept. Though the "man of sin" succeeded in trampling underfoot God's holy day, yet even in the period of his supremacy there were, hidden in secret places, faithful souls who paid it honor. Since the Reformation, there have been some in every generation to maintain its observance. Though often in the midst of reproach and persecution, a constant testimony has been borne to the perpetuity of the law of God and the sacred obligation of the creation Sabbath.

These truths, as presented in Revelation 14 in connection with "the everlasting gospel," will distinguish the church of Christ at the time of His appearing. For as the result of the threefold message it is announced: "Here are they that keep the commandments of God, and the faith of Jesus." And this message is the last to be given before the coming of the Lord. Immediately following its proclamation the Son of man is seen by the prophet, coming in glory to reap the harvest of the earth.

Those who received the light concerning the sanctuary and the immutability of the law of God were filled with joy and wonder as they saw the beauty and harmony of the system of truth that opened to their understanding. They desired that the light which appeared to them so precious might be imparted to all Christians; and they could not but believe that it would be joyfully accepted. But truths that would place them at variance with the world were not welcome to many who claimed to be followers of Christ. Obedience to the fourth commandment required a sacrifice from which the majority drew back.

As the claims of the Sabbath were presented, many reasoned from the worldling's standpoint. Said they: "We have always kept Sunday, our fathers kept it, and many good and pious men have died happy while keeping it. If they were right, so are we. The keeping of this new Sabbath would throw us out of harmony with the world, and we would have no influence over them. What can a little company keeping the seventh day hope to accomplish against all the world who are keeping Sunday?" It was by similar arguments that the Jews endeavored to justify their rejection of Christ. Their fathers had been accepted of God in presenting the sacrificial offerings, and why could not the children find salvation in pursuing the same course? So, in the time of Luther, papists reasoned that true Christians had died in the Catholic faith, and therefore that religion was sufficient for salvation. Such reasoning would prove an effectual barrier to all advancement in religious faith or practice.

Many urged that Sundaykeeping had been an established doctrine and a widespread custom of the church for many centuries. Against this argument it was shown that the Sabbath and its observance were more ancient and widespread, even as old as the world itself, and bearing the sanction both of angels and of God. When the foundations of the earth were laid, when the morning stars sang together, and all the sons of God shouted for joy, then was laid the foundation of the Sabbath. Job 38:6, 7; Genesis 2:1-3. Well may this institution demand our reverence; it was ordained by no human authority and rests upon no human traditions; it was established by the Ancient of Days and commanded by His eternal word.

As the attention of the people was called to the subject of Sabbath reform, popular ministers perverted the word of God, placing such interpretations upon its testimony as would best quiet inquiring minds. And those who did not search the Scriptures for themselves were content to accept conclusions that were in accordance with their desires. By argument, sophistry, the traditions of the Fathers, and the authority of the church, many endeavored to overthrow the truth. Its advocates were driven to their Bibles to defend the validity of the fourth commandment. Humble men, armed with the word of truth alone, withstood the attacks of men of learning, who, with surprise and anger, found their eloquent sophistry powerless against the simple, straightforward reasoning of men who were versed in the Scriptures rather than in the subtleties of the schools.

In the absence of Bible testimony in their favor, many with unwearying persistence urged—forgetting how the same reasoning had been employed against Christ and His apostles: "Why do not our great men understand this Sabbath question? But few believe as you do. It cannot be that you are right and that all the men of learning in the world are wrong."

To refute such arguments it was needful only to cite the teachings of the Scriptures and the history of the Lord's dealings with His people in all ages. God works through those who hear and obey His voice, those who will, if need be, speak unpalatable truths, those who do not fear to reprove popular sins. The reason why He does not oftener choose men of learning and high position to lead out in reform movements is that they trust to their creeds, theories, and theological systems, and feel no need to be taught of God. Only those who have a personal connection with the Source of wisdom are able to understand or explain the Scriptures. Men who have little of the learning of the schools are sometimes called to declare the truth, not because they are unlearned, but because they are not too self-sufficient to be taught of God. They learn in the school of Christ, and their humility and obedience make them great. In committing to them a knowledge of His truth, God confers upon them an honor, in comparison with which earthly honor and human greatness sink into insignificance.

The majority of Adventists rejected the truths concerning the sanctuary and the law of God, and many also renounced their faith in the advent movement and adopted unsound and conflicting views of the prophecies which applied to that work. Some were led into the error of repeatedly fixing upon a definite time for the coming of Christ. The light which was now shining on the subject of the sanctuary should have shown them that no prophetic period extends to the second advent; that the exact time of this advent is not foretold. But, turning from the light, they continued to set time after time for the Lord to come, and as often they were disappointed.

When the Thessalonian church received erroneous views concerning the coming of Christ, the apostle Paul counseled them to test their hopes and anticipations carefully by the word of God. He cited them to prophecies revealing the events to take place before Christ should come, and showed that they had no ground to expect Him in their day. "Let no man deceive you by any means" (2 Thessalonians 2:3), are his words of warning. Should they indulge expectations that were not sanctioned by the Scriptures, they would be led to a mistaken course of action; disappointment would expose them to the derision of unbelievers, and they would be in danger of yielding to discouragement and would be tempted to doubt the truths essential for their salvation. The apostle's admonition to the Thessalonians contains an important lesson for those who live in the last days. Many Adventists have felt that unless they could fix their faith upon a definite time for the Lord's coming, they could not be zealous and diligent in the work of preparation. But as their hopes are again and again excited, only to be destroyed, their faith receives such a shock that it becomes well-nigh impossible for them to be impressed by the great truths of prophecy.

The preaching of a definite time for the judgment, in the giving of the first message, was ordered by God. The computation of the prophetic periods on which that message was based, placing the close of the 2300 days in the autumn of 1844, stands without impeachment. The repeated efforts to find new dates for the beginning and close of the prophetic periods, and the unsound reasoning necessary to sustain these positions, not only lead minds away from the present truth, but throw contempt upon all efforts to explain the prophecies. The more frequently a definite time is set for the second advent, and the more widely it is taught, the better it suits the purposes of Satan. After the time has passed, he excites ridicule and contempt of its advocates, and thus casts reproach upon the great advent movement of 1843 and 1844. Those who persist in this error will at last fix upon a date too far in the future for the coming of Christ. Thus they will be led to rest in a false security, and many will not be undeceived until it is too late.

The history of ancient Israel is a striking illustration of the past experience of the Adventist body. God led His people in the advent movement, even as He led the children of Israel from Egypt. In the great disappointment their faith was tested as was that of the Hebrews at the Red Sea. Had they still trusted to the guiding hand that had been with them in their past experience, they would have seen the salvation of God. If all who had labored unitedly in the work in 1844, had received the third angel's message and proclaimed it in the power of the Holy Spirit, the Lord would have wrought mightily with their efforts. A flood of light would have been shed upon the world. Years ago the inhabitants of the earth would have been warned, the closing work completed, and Christ would have come for the redemption of His people.

It was not the will of God that Israel should wander forty years in the wilderness; He desired to lead them directly to the land of Canaan and establish them there, a holy, happy people. But "they could not enter in because of unbelief." Hebrews 3:19. Because of their backsliding and apostasy they perished in the desert, and others were raised up to enter the Promised Land. In like manner, it was not the will of God that the coming of Christ should be so long delayed and His people should remain so many years in this world of sin and sorrow. But unbelief separated them from God. As they refused to do the work which He had appointed them, others were raised up to proclaim the message. In mercy to the world, Jesus delays His coming, that sinners may have an opportunity to hear the warning and find in Him a shelter before the wrath of God shall be poured out.

Now as in former ages, the presentation of a truth that reproves the sins and errors of the times will excite opposition. "Everyone that doeth evil hateth the light, neither cometh to the light, lest his deeds should be reproved." John 3:20. As men see that they cannot maintain their position by the Scriptures, many determine to maintain it at all hazards, and with a malicious spirit they assail the character and motives of those who stand in defense of unpopular truth. It is the same policy which has been pursued in all ages. Elijah was declared to be a troubler in Israel, Jeremiah a traitor, Paul a polluter of the temple. From that day to this, those who would be loyal to truth have been denounced as seditious, heretical, or schismatic. Multitudes who are too unbelieving to accept the sure word of prophecy will receive with unquestioning credulity an accusation against those who dare to reprove fashionable sins. This spirit will increase more and more. And the Bible plainly teaches that a time is approaching when the laws of the state will so conflict with the law of God that whosoever would obey all the divine precepts must brave reproach and punishment as an evildoer.

In view of this, what is the duty of the messenger of truth? Shall he conclude that the truth ought not to be presented, since often its only effect is to arouse men to evade or resist its claims? No; he has no more reason for withholding the testimony of God's word, because it excites opposition, than had earlier Reformers. The confession of faith made by saints and martyrs was recorded for the benefit of succeeding generations. Those living examples of holiness and steadfast integrity have come down to inspire courage in those who are now called to stand as witnesses for God. They received grace and truth, not for themselves alone, but that, through them, the knowledge of God might enlighten the earth. Has God given light to His servants in this generation? Then they should let it shine forth to the world.

Anciently the Lord declared to one who spoke in His name: "The house of Israel will not hearken unto thee; for they will not hearken unto Me." Nevertheless He said: "Thou shalt speak My words unto them, whether they will hear, or whether they will forbear." Ezekiel 3:7; 2:7. To the servant of God at this time is the command addressed: "Lift up thy voice like a trumpet, and show My people their transgression, and the house of Jacob their sins."

So far as his opportunities extend, everyone who has received the light of truth is under the same solemn and fearful responsibility as was the prophet of Israel, to whom the word of the Lord came, saying: "Son of man, I have set thee a watchman unto the house of Israel; therefore thou shalt hear the word at My mouth, and warn them from Me. When I say unto the wicked, O wicked man, thou shalt surely die; if thou dost not speak to warn the wicked from his way, that wicked man shall die in his iniquity; but his blood will I require at thine hand. Nevertheless, if thou warn the wicked of his way to turn from it; if he do not turn from his way, he shall die in his iniquity; but thou hast delivered thy soul." Ezekiel 33:7-9.

The great obstacle both to the acceptance and to the promulgation of truth is the fact that it involves inconvenience and reproach. This is the only argument against the truth which its advocates have never been able to refute. But this does not deter the true followers of Christ. These do not wait for truth to become popular. Being convinced of their duty, they deliberately accept the cross, with the apostle Paul counting that "our light affliction, which is but for a moment, worketh for us a far more exceeding and eternal weight of glory;" with one of old, "esteeming the reproach of Christ greater riches than the treasures in Egypt." 2 Corinthians 4:17; Hebrews 11:26.

Whatever may be their profession, it is only those who are world servers at heart that act from policy rather than principle in religious things. We should choose the right because it is right, and leave consequences with God. To men of principle, faith, and daring, the world is indebted for its great reforms. By such men the work of reform for this time must be carried forward.

Thus saith the Lord: "Hearken unto Me, ye that know righteousness, the people in whose heart is My law; fear ye not the reproach of men, neither be ye afraid of their revilings. For the moth shall eat them up like a garment, and the worm shall eat them like wool: but My righteousness shall be forever, and My salvation from generation to generation." Isaiah 51:7, 8.

Five

—The Final Warning—

"I saw another angel come down from heaven, having great power; and the earth was lightened with his glory. And he cried mightily with a strong voice, saying, Babylon the great is fallen, is fallen, and is become the habitation of devils, and the hold of every foul spirit, and a cage of every unclean and hateful bird." "And I heard another voice from heaven, saying, Come out of her, My people, that ye be not partakers of her sins, and that ye receive not of her plagues." Revelation 18:1, 2, 4.

This scripture points forward to a time when the announcement of the fall of Babylon, as made by the second angel of Revelation 14 (verse 8), is to be repeated, with the additional mention of the corruptions which have been entering the various organizations that constitute Babylon, since that message was first given, in the summer of 1844. A terrible condition of the religious world is here described. With every rejection of truth the minds of the people will become darker, their hearts more stubborn, until they are entrenched in an infidel hardihood. In defiance of the warnings which God has given, they will continue to trample upon one of the precepts of the Decalogue, until they are led to persecute those who hold it sacred. Christ is set at nought in the contempt placed upon His word and His people. As the teachings of spiritualism are accepted by the churches, the restraint imposed upon the carnal heart is removed, and the profession of religion will become a cloak to conceal the basest iniquity. A belief in spiritual manifestations opens the door to seducing spirits and doctrines of devils, and thus the influence of evil angels will be felt in the churches.

Of Babylon, at the time brought to view in this prophecy, it is declared: "Her sins have reached unto heaven, and God hath remembered her iniquities." Revelation 18:5. She has filled up the measure of her guilt, and destruction is about to fall upon her. But God still has a people in Babylon; and before the visitation of His judgments these faithful ones must be called out, that they partake not of her sins and "receive not of her plagues." Hence the movement symbolized by the angel coming down from heaven, lightening the earth with his glory and crying mightily with a strong voice, announcing the sins of Babylon. In connection with his message the call is heard: "Come out of her, My people." These announcements, uniting with the third angel's message, constitute the final warning to be given to the inhabitants of the earth.

Fearful is the issue to which the world is to be brought. The powers of earth, uniting to war against the commandments of God, will decree that "all, both small and great, rich and poor, free and bond" (Revelation 13:16), shall conform to the customs of the church by the observance of the false sabbath. All who refuse compliance will be visited with civil penalties, and it will finally be declared that they are deserving of death. On the other hand, the law of God enjoining the Creator's rest day demands obedience and threatens wrath against all who transgress its precepts.

With the issue thus clearly brought before him, whoever shall trample upon God's law to obey a human enactment receives the mark of the beast; he accepts the sign of allegiance to the power which he chooses to obey instead of God. The warning from heaven is: "If any man worship the beast and his image, and receive his mark in his forehead, or in his hand, the same shall drink of the wine of the wrath of God, which is poured out without mixture into the cup of His indignation." Revelation 14:9, 10.

But not one is made to suffer the wrath of God until the truth has been brought home to his mind and conscience, and has been rejected. There are many who have never had an opportunity to hear the special truths for this time. The obligation of the fourth commandment has never been set before them in its true light. He who reads every heart and tries every motive will leave none who desire a knowledge of the truth, to be deceived as to the issues of the controversy. The decree is not to be urged upon the people blindly. Everyone is to have sufficient light to make his decision intelligently.

The Sabbath will be the great test of loyalty, for it is the point of truth especially controverted. When the final test shall be brought to bear upon men, then the line of distinction will be drawn between those who serve God and those who serve Him not. While the observance of the false sabbath in compliance with the law of the state, contrary to the fourth commandment, will be an avowal of allegiance to a power that is in opposition to God, the keeping of the true Sabbath, in obedience to God's law, is an evidence of loyalty to the Creator. While one class, by accepting the sign of submission to earthly powers, receive the mark of the beast, the other choosing the token of allegiance to divine authority, receive the seal of God.

Heretofore those who presented the truths of the third angel's message have often been regarded as mere alarmists. Their predictions that religious intolerance would gain control in the United States, that church and state would unite to persecute those who keep the commandments of God, have been pronounced groundless and absurd. It has been confidently declared that this land could never become other than what it has been—the defender of religious freedom. But as the question of enforcing Sunday observance is widely agitated, the event so long doubted and disbelieved is seen to be approaching, and the third message will produce an effect which it could not have had before.

In every generation God has sent His servants to rebuke sin, both in the world and in the church. But the people desire smooth things spoken to them, and the pure, unvarnished truth is not acceptable. Many reformers, in entering upon their work, determined to exercise great prudence in attacking the sins of the church and the nation. They hoped, by the example of a pure Christian life, to lead the people back to the doctrines of the Bible. But the Spirit of God came upon them as it came upon Elijah, moving him to rebuke the sins of a wicked king and an apostate people; they could not refrain from preaching the plain utterances of the Bible—doctrines which they had been reluctant to present. They were impelled to zealously declare the truth and the danger which threatened souls. The words which the Lord gave them they uttered, fearless of consequences, and the people were compelled to hear the warning.

Thus the message of the third angel will be proclaimed. As the time comes for it to be given with greatest power, the Lord will work through humble instruments, leading the minds of those who consecrate themselves to His service. The laborers will be qualified rather by the unction of His Spirit than by the training of literary institutions.

Men of faith and prayer will be constrained to go forth with holy zeal, declaring the words which God gives them. The sins of Babylon will be laid open. The fearful results of enforcing the observances of the church by civil authority, the inroads of spiritualism, the stealthy but rapid progress of the papal power—all will be unmasked. By these solemn warnings the people will be stirred. Thousands upon thousands will listen who have never heard words like these. In amazement they hear the testimony that Babylon is the church, fallen because of her errors and sins, because of her rejection of the truth sent to her from heaven. As the people go to their former teachers with the eager inquiry, Are these things so? the ministers present fables, prophesy smooth things, to soothe their fears and quiet the awakened conscience. But since many refuse to be satisfied with the mere authority of men and demand a plain "Thus saith the Lord," the popular ministry, like the Pharisees of old, filled with anger as their authority is questioned, will denounce the message as of Satan and stir up the sin-loving multitudes to revile and persecute those who proclaim it.

As the controversy extends into new fields and the minds of the people are called to God's downtrodden law, Satan is astir. The power attending the message will only madden those who oppose it. The clergy will put forth almost superhuman efforts to shut away the light lest it should shine upon their flocks. By every means at their command they will endeavor to suppress the discussion of these vital questions. The church appeals to the strong arm of civil power, and, in this work, papists and Protestants unite. As the movement for Sunday enforcement becomes more bold and decided, the law will be invoked against commandment keepers. They will be threatened with fines and imprisonment, and some will be offered positions of influence, and other rewards and advantages, as inducements to renounce their faith. But their steadfast answer is: "Show us from the word of God our error"—the same plea that was made by Luther under similar circumstances. Those who are arraigned before the courts make a strong vindication of the truth, and some who hear them are led to take their stand to keep all the commandments of God. Thus light will be brought before thousands who otherwise would know nothing of these truths.

Conscientious obedience to the word of God will be treated as rebellion. Blinded by Satan, the parent will exercise harshness and severity toward the believing child; the master or mistress will oppress the commandment-keeping servant. Affection will be alienated; children will be disinherited and driven from home. The words of Paul will be literally fulfilled: "All that will live godly in Christ Jesus shall suffer persecution." 2 Timothy 3:12. As the defenders of truth refuse to honor the Sunday-sabbath, some of them will be thrust into prison, some will be exiled, some will be treated as slaves. To human wisdom all this now seems impossible; but as the restraining Spirit of God shall be withdrawn from men, and they shall be under the control of Satan, who hates the divine precepts, there will be strange developments. The heart can be very cruel when God's fear and love are removed.

As the storm approaches, a large class who have professed faith in the third angel's message, but have not been sanctified through obedience to the truth, abandon their position and join the ranks of the opposition. By uniting with the world and partaking of its spirit, they have come to view matters in nearly the same light; and when the test is brought, they are prepared to choose the easy, popular side. Men of talent and pleasing address, who once rejoiced in the truth, employ their powers to deceive and mislead souls. They become the most bitter enemies of their former brethren. When Sabbathkeepers are brought before the courts to answer for their faith, these apostates are the most efficient agents of Satan to misrepresent and accuse them, and by false reports and insinuations to stir up the rulers against them.

In this time of persecution the faith of the Lord's servants will be tried. They have faithfully given the warning, looking to God and to His word alone. God's Spirit, moving upon their hearts, has constrained them to speak. Stimulated with holy zeal, and with the divine impulse strong upon them, they entered upon the performance of their duties without coldly calculating the consequences of speaking to the people the word which the Lord had given them. They have not consulted their temporal interests, nor sought to preserve their reputation or their lives. Yet when the storm of opposition and reproach bursts upon them, some, overwhelmed with consternation, will be ready to exclaim: "Had we foreseen the consequences of our words, we would have held our peace." They are hedged in with difficulties. Satan assails them with fierce temptations. The work which they have undertaken seems far beyond their ability to accomplish. They are threatened with destruction. The enthusiasm which animated them is gone; yet they cannot turn back. Then, feeling their utter helplessness, they flee to the Mighty One for strength. They remember that the words which they have spoken were not theirs, but His who bade them give the warning. God put the truth into their hearts, and they could not forbear to proclaim it.

The same trials have been experienced by men of God in ages past. Wycliffe, Huss, Luther, Tyndale, Baxter, Wesley, urged that all doctrines be brought to the test of the Bible and declared that they would renounce everything which it condemned. Against these men persecution raged with relentless fury; yet they ceased not to declare the truth. Different periods in the history of the church have each been marked by the development of some special truth, adapted to the necessities of God's people at that time. Every new truth has made its way against hatred and opposition; those who were blessed with its light were tempted and tried. The Lord gives a special truth for the people in an emergency. Who dare refuse to publish it? He commands His servants to present the last invitation of mercy to the world. They cannot remain silent, except at the peril of their souls. Christ's ambassadors have nothing to do with consequences. They must perform their duty and leave results with God.

As the opposition rises to a fiercer height, the servants of God are again perplexed; for it seems to them that they have brought the crisis. But conscience and the word of God assure them that their course is right; and although the trials continue, they are strengthened to bear them. The contest grows closer and sharper, but their faith and courage rise with the emergency. Their testimony is: "We dare not tamper with God's word, dividing His holy law; calling one portion essential and another nonessential, to gain the favor of the world. The Lord whom we serve is able to deliver us. Christ has conquered the powers of earth; and shall we be afraid of a world already conquered?"

Persecution in its varied forms is the development of a principle which will exist as long as Satan exists and Christianity has vital power. No man can serve God without enlisting against himself the opposition of the hosts of darkness. Evil angels will assail him, alarmed that his influence is taking the prey from their hands. Evil men, rebuked by his example, will unite with them in seeking to separate him from God by alluring temptations. When these do not succeed, then a compelling power is employed to force the conscience.

But so long as Jesus remains man's intercessor in the sanctuary above, the restraining influence of the Holy Spirit is felt by rulers and people. It still controls to some extent the laws of the land. Were it not for these laws, the condition of the world would be much worse than it now is. While many of our rulers are active agents of Satan, God also has His agents among the leading men of the nation. The enemy moves upon his servants to propose measures that would greatly impede the work of God; but statesmen who fear the Lord are influenced by holy angels to oppose such propositions with unanswerable arguments. Thus a few men will hold in check a powerful current of evil. The opposition of the enemies of truth will be restrained that the third angel's message may do its work. When the final warning shall be given, it will arrest the attention of these leading men through whom the Lord is now working, and some of them will accept it, and will stand with the people of God through the time of trouble.

The angel who unites in the proclamation of the third angel's message is to lighten the whole earth with his glory. A work of worldwide extent and unwonted power is here foretold. The advent movement of 1840-44 was a glorious manifestation of the power of God; the first angel's message was carried to every missionary station in the world, and in some countries there was the greatest religious interest which has been witnessed in any land since the Reformation of the sixteenth century; but these are to be exceeded by the mighty movement under the last warning of the third angel.

The work will be similar to that of the Day of Pentecost. As the "former rain" was given, in the outpouring of the Holy Spirit at the opening of the gospel, to cause the upspringing of the precious seed, so the "latter rain" will be given at its close for the ripening of the harvest. "Then shall we know, if we follow on to know the Lord: His going forth is prepared as the morning; and He shall come unto us as the rain, as the latter and former rain unto the earth." Hosea 6:3. "Be glad then, ye children of Zion, and rejoice in the Lord your God: for He hath given you the former rain moderately, and He will cause to come down for you the rain, the former rain, and the latter rain." Joel 2:23. "In the last days, saith God, I will pour out of My Spirit upon all flesh." "And it shall come to pass, that whosoever shall call on the name of the Lord shall be saved." Acts 2:17, 21.

The great work of the gospel is not to close with less manifestation of the power of God than marked its opening. The prophecies which were fulfilled in the outpouring of the former rain at the opening of the gospel are again to be fulfilled in the latter rain at its close. Here are "the times of refreshing" to which the apostle Peter looked forward when he said: "Repent ye therefore, and be converted, that your sins may be blotted out, when the times of refreshing shall come from the presence of the Lord; and He shall send Jesus." Acts 3:19, 20.

Servants of God, with their faces lighted up and shining with holy consecration, will hasten from place to place to proclaim the message from heaven. By thousands of voices, all over the earth, the warning will be given. Miracles will be wrought, the sick will be healed, and signs and wonders will follow the believers. Satan also works, with lying wonders, even bringing down fire from heaven in the sight of men. Revelation 13:13. Thus the inhabitants of the earth will be brought to take their stand.

The message will be carried not so much by argument as by the deep conviction of the Spirit of God. The arguments have been presented. The seed has been sown, and now it will spring up and bear fruit. The publications distributed by missionary workers have exerted their influence, yet many whose minds were impressed have been prevented from fully comprehending the truth or from yielding obedience. Now the rays of light penetrate everywhere, the truth is seen in its clearness, and the honest children of God sever the bands which have held them. Family connections, church relations, are powerless to stay them now. Truth is more precious than all besides. Notwithstanding the agencies combined against the truth, a large number take their stand upon the Lord's side.

Six

—Facing Life's Record—

"I beheld," says the prophet Daniel, "till thrones were placed, and One that was Ancient of Days did sit: His raiment was white as snow, and the hair of His head like pure wool; His throne was fiery flames, and the wheels thereof burning fire. A fiery stream issued and came forth from before Him: thousand thousands ministered unto Him, and ten thousand times ten thousand stood before Him: the judgment was set, and the books were opened." Daniel 7:9, 10, R.V.

Thus was presented to the prophet's vision the great and solemn day when the characters and the lives of men should pass in review before the Judge of all the earth, and to every man should be rendered "according to his works." The Ancient of Days is God the Father. Says the psalmist: "Before the mountains were brought forth, or ever Thou hadst formed the earth and the world, even from everlasting to everlasting, Thou art God." Psalm 90:2. It is He, the source of all being, and the fountain of all law, that is to preside in the judgment. And holy angels as ministers and witnesses, in number "ten thousand times ten thousand, and thousands of thousands," attend this great tribunal.

"And, behold, one like the Son of man came with the clouds of heaven, and came to the Ancient of Days, and they brought Him near before Him. And there was given Him dominion, and glory, and a kingdom, that all people, nations, and languages, should serve Him: His dominion is an everlasting dominion, which shall not pass away." Daniel 7:13, 14. The coming of Christ here described is not His second coming to the earth. He comes to the Ancient of Days in heaven to receive dominion and glory and a kingdom, which will be given Him at the close of His work as a mediator. It is this coming, and not His second advent to the earth, that was foretold in prophecy to take place at the termination of the 2300 days in 1844. Attended by heavenly angels, our great High Priest enters the holy of holies and there appears in the presence of God to engage in the last acts of His ministration in behalf of man—to perform the work of investigative judgment and to make an atonement for all who are shown to be entitled to its benefits.

In the typical service only those who had come before God with confession and repentance, and whose sins, through the blood of the sin offering, were transferred to the sanctuary, had a part in the service of the Day of Atonement. So in the great day of final atonement and investigative judgment the only cases considered are those of the professed people of God. The judgment of the wicked is a distinct and separate work, and takes place at a later period. "Judgment must begin at the house of God: and if it first begin at us, what shall the end be of them that obey not the gospel?" 1 Peter 4:17.

The books of record in heaven, in which the names and the deeds of men are registered, are to determine the decisions of the judgment. Says the prophet Daniel: "The judgment was set, and the books were opened." The revelator, describing the same scene, adds: "Another book was opened, which is the book of life: and the dead were judged out of those things which were written in the books, according to their works." Revelation 20:12.

The book of life contains the names of all who have ever entered the service of God. Jesus bade His disciples: "Rejoice, because your names are written in heaven." Luke 10:20. Paul speaks of his faithful fellow workers, "whose names are in the book of life." Philippians 4:3. Daniel, looking down to "a time of trouble, such as never was," declares that God's people shall be delivered, "everyone that shall be found written in the book." And the revelator says that those only shall enter the city of God whose names "are written in the Lamb's book of life." Daniel 12:1; Revelation 21:27.

"A book of remembrance" is written before God, in which are recorded the good deeds of "them that feared the Lord, and that thought upon His name." Malachi 3:16. Their words of faith, their acts of love, are registered in heaven. Nehemiah refers to this when he says: "Remember me, O my God, ... and wipe not out my good deeds that I have done for the house of my God." Nehemiah 13:14. In the book of God's remembrance every deed of righteousness is immortalized. There every temptation resisted, every evil overcome, every word of tender pity expressed, is faithfully chronicled. And every act of sacrifice, every suffering and sorrow endured for Christ's sake, is recorded. Says the psalmist: "Thou tellest my wanderings: put Thou my tears into Thy bottle: are they not in Thy book?" Psalm 56:8.

There is a record also of the sins of men. "For God shall bring every work into judgment, with every secret thing, whether it be good, or whether it be evil." Every idle word that men shall speak, they shall give account thereof in the day of judgment." Says the Saviour: "By thy words thou shalt be justified, and by thy words thou shalt be condemned." Ecclesiastes 12:14; Matthew 12:36, 37. The secret purposes and motives appear in the unerring register; for God "will bring to light the hidden things of darkness, and will make manifest the counsels of the hearts." I Corinthians 4:5. "Behold, it is written before Me, ... your iniquities, and the iniquities of your fathers together, saith the Lord." Isaiah 65:6, 7.

Every man's work passes in review before God and is registered for faithfulness or unfaithfulness. Opposite each name in the books of heaven is entered with terrible exactness every wrong word, every selfish act, every unfulfilled duty, and every secret sin, with every artful dissembling. Heaven-sent warnings or reproofs neglected, wasted moments, unimproved opportunities, the influence exerted for good or for evil, with its far-reaching results, all are chronicled by the recording angel.

The law of God is the standard by which the characters and the lives of men will be tested in the judgment. Says the wise man: "Fear God, and keep His commandments: for this is the whole duty of man. For God shall bring every work into judgment." Ecclesiastes 12:13, 14. The apostle James admonishes his brethren: "So speak ye, and so do, as they that shall be judged by the law of liberty." James 2:12

Those who in the judgment are "accounted worthy" will have a part in the resurrection of the just. Jesus said: "They which shall be accounted worthy to obtain that world, and the resurrection from the dead, ... are equal unto the angels; and are the children of God, being the children of the resurrection." Luke 20:35, 36. And again He declares that "they that have done good" shall come forth "unto the resurrection of life." John 5:29. The righteous dead will not be raised until after the judgment at which they are accounted worthy of "the resurrection of life." Hence they will not be present in person at the tribunal when their records are examined and their cases decided.

Jesus will appear as their advocate, to plead in their behalf before God. "If any man sin, we have an advocate with the Father, Jesus Christ the righteous." I John 2:1. "For Christ is not entered into the holy places made with hands, which are the figures of the true; but into heaven itself, now to appear in the presence of God for us." "Wherefore He is able also to save them to the uttermost that come unto God by Him, seeing He ever liveth to make intercession for them." Hebrews 9:24; 7:25.

As the books of record are opened in the judgment, the lives of all who have believed on Jesus come in review before God. Beginning with those who first lived upon the earth, our Advocate presents the cases of each successive generation, and closes with the living. Every name is mentioned, every case closely investigated. Names are accepted, names rejected. When any have sins remaining upon the books of record, unrepented of and unforgiven, their names will be blotted out of the book of life, and the record of their good deeds will be erased from the book of God's remembrance. The Lord declared to Moses: "Whosoever hath sinned against Me, him will I blot out of My book." Exodus 32:33. And says the prophet Ezekiel: "When the righteous turneth away from his righteousness, and committeth iniquity, … all his righteousness that he hath done shall not be mentioned." Ezekiel 18:24.

All who have truly repented of sin, and by faith claimed the blood of Christ as their atoning sacrifice, have had pardon entered against their names in the books of heaven; as they have become partakers of the righteousness of Christ, and their characters are found to be in harmony with the law of God, their sins will be blotted out, and they themselves will be accounted worthy of eternal life. The Lord declares, by the prophet Isaiah: "I, even I, am He that blotteth out thy transgressions for Mine own sake, and will not remember thy sins." Isaiah 43:25. Said Jesus: "He that overcometh, the same shall be clothed in white raiment; and I will not blot out his name out of the book of life, but I will confess his name before My Father, and before His angels." "Whosoever therefore shall confess Me before men, him will I confess also before My Father which is in heaven. But whosoever shall deny Me before men, him will I also deny before My Father which is in heaven." Revelation 3:5; Matthew 10:32, 33.

The deepest interest manifested among men in the decisions of earthly tribunals but faintly represents the interest evinced in the heavenly courts when the names entered in the book of life come up in review before the Judge of all the earth. The divine Intercessor presents the plea that all who have overcome through faith in His blood be forgiven their transgressions, that they be restored to their Eden home, and crowned as joint heirs with Himself to "the first dominion." Micah 4:8. Satan in his efforts to deceive and tempt our race had thought to frustrate the divine plan in man's creation; but Christ now asks that this plan be carried into effect as if man had never fallen. He asks for His people not only pardon and justification, full and complete, but a share in His glory and a seat upon His throne.

While Jesus is pleading for the subjects of His grace, Satan accuses them before God as transgressors. The great deceiver has sought to lead them into skepticism, to cause them to lose confidence in God, to separate themselves from His love, and to break His law. Now he points to the record of their lives, to the defects of character, the unlikeness to Christ, which has dishonored their Redeemer, to all the sins that he has tempted them to commit, and because of these he claims them as his subjects.

Jesus does not excuse their sins, but shows their penitence and faith, and, claiming for them forgiveness, He lifts His wounded hands before the Father and the holy angels, saying: I know them by name. I have graven them on the palms of My hands. "The sacrifices of God are a broken spirit: a broken and a contrite heart, O God, Thou wilt not despise." Psalm 51:17. And to the accuser of His people He declares: "The Lord rebuke thee, O Satan; even the Lord that hath chosen Jerusalem rebuke thee: is not this a brand plucked out of the fire?" Zechariah 3:2. Christ will clothe His faithful ones with His own righteousness, that He may present them to His Father "a glorious church, not having spot, or wrinkle, or any such thing." Ephesians 5:27. Their names stand enrolled in the book of life, and concerning them it is written: "They shall walk with Me in white: for they are worthy." Revelation 3:4.

Thus will be realized the complete fulfillment of the new-covenant promise: "I will forgive their iniquity, and I will remember their sin no more." "In those days, and in that time, saith the Lord, the iniquity of Israel shall be sought for, and there shall be none; and the sins of Judah, and they shall not be found." Jeremiah 31:34; 50:20. "In that day shall the branch of the Lord be beautiful and glorious, and the fruit of the earth shall be excellent and comely for them that are escaped of Israel. And it shall come to pass, that he that is left in Zion, and he that remaineth in Jerusalem, shall be called holy, even everyone that is written among the living in Jerusalem." Isaiah 4:2, 3.

The work of the investigative judgment and the blotting out of sins is to be accomplished before the second advent of the Lord. Since the dead are to be judged out of the things written in the books, it is impossible that the sins of men should be blotted out until after the judgment at which their cases are to be investigated. But the apostle Peter distinctly states that the sins of believers will be blotted out "when the times of refreshing shall come from the presence of the Lord; and He shall send Jesus Christ." Acts 3:19, 20. When the investigative judgment closes, Christ will come, and His reward will be with Him to give to every man as his work shall be.

In the typical service the high priest, having made the atonement for Israel, came forth and blessed the congregation. So Christ, at the close of His work as mediator, will appear, "without sin unto salvation" (Hebrews 9:28), to bless His waiting people with eternal life. As the priest, in removing the sins from the sanctuary, confessed them upon the head of the scapegoat, so Christ will place all these sins upon Satan, the originator and instigator of sin. The scapegoat, bearing the sins of Israel, was sent away "unto a land not inhabited" (Leviticus 16:22); so Satan, bearing the guilt of all the sins which he has caused God's people to commit, will be for a thousand years confined to the earth, which will then be desolate, without inhabitant, and he will at last suffer the full penalty of sin in the fires that shall destroy all the wicked. Thus the great plan of redemption will reach its accomplishment in the final eradication of sin and the deliverance of all who have been willing to renounce evil.

At the time appointed for the judgment—the close of the 2300 days, in 1844—began the work of investigation and blotting out of sins. All who have ever taken upon themselves the name of Christ must pass its searching scrutiny. Both the living and the dead are to be judged "out of those things which were written in the books, according to their works."

Sins that have not been repented of and forsaken will not be pardoned and blotted out of the books of record, but will stand to witness against the sinner in the day of God. He may have committed his evil deeds in the light of day or in the darkness of night; but they were open and manifest before Him with whom we have to do. Angels of God witnessed each sin and registered it in the unerring records. Sin may be concealed, denied, covered up from father, mother, wife, children, and associates; no one but the guilty actors may cherish the least suspicion of the wrong; but it is laid bare before the intelligences of heaven. The darkness of the darkest night, the secrecy of all deceptive arts, is not sufficient to veil one thought from the knowledge of the Eternal. God has an exact record of every unjust account and every unfair dealing. He is not deceived by appearances of piety. He makes no mistakes in His estimation of character. Men may be deceived by those who are corrupt in heart, but God pierces all disguises and reads the inner life.

How solemn is the thought! Day after day, passing into eternity, bears its burden of records for the books of heaven. Words once spoken, deeds once done, can never be recalled. Angels have registered both the good and the evil. The mightiest conqueror upon the earth cannot call back the record of even a single day. Our acts, our words, even our most secret motives, all have their weight in deciding our destiny for weal or woe. Though they may be forgotten by us, they will bear their testimony to justify or condemn.

As the features of the countenance are reproduced with unerring accuracy on the polished plate of the artist, so the character is faithfully delineated in the books above. Yet how little solicitude is felt concerning that record which is to meet the gaze of heavenly beings. Could the veil which separates the visible from the invisible world be swept back, and the children of men behold an angel recording every word and deed, which they must meet again in the judgment, how many words that are daily uttered would remain unspoken, how many deeds would remain undone.

In the judgment the use made of every talent will be scrutinized. How have we employed the capital lent us of Heaven? Will the Lord at His coming receive His own with usury? Have we improved the powers entrusted us, in hand and heart and brain, to the glory of God and the blessing of the world? How have we used our time, our pen, our voice, our money, our influence? What have we done for Christ, in the person of the poor, the afflicted, the orphan, or the widow? God has made us the depositaries of His holy word; what have we done with the light and truth given us to make men wise unto salvation? No value is attached to a mere profession of faith in Christ; only the love which is shown by works is counted genuine. Yet it is love alone which in the sight of Heaven makes any act of value. Whatever is done from love, however small it may appear in the estimation of men, is accepted and rewarded of God.

The hidden selfishness of men stands revealed in the books of heaven. There is the record of unfulfilled duties to their fellow men, of forgetfulness of the Saviour's claims. There they will see how often were given to Satan the time, thought, and strength that belonged to Christ. Sad is the record which angels bear to heaven. Intelligent beings, professed followers of Christ, are absorbed in the acquirement of worldly possessions or the enjoyment of earthly pleasures. Money, time, and strength are sacrificed for display and self-indulgence; but few are the moments devoted to prayer, to the searching of the Scriptures, to humiliation of soul and confession of sin.

Satan invents unnumbered schemes to occupy our minds, that they may not dwell upon the very work with which we ought to be best acquainted. The archdeceiver hates the great truths that bring to view an atoning sacrifice and an all-powerful mediator. He knows that with him everything depends on his diverting minds from Jesus and His truth.

Those who would share the benefits of the Saviour's mediation should permit nothing to interfere with their duty to perfect holiness in the fear of God. The precious hours, instead of being given to pleasure, to display, or to gain seeking, should be devoted to an earnest, prayerful study of the word of truth. The subject of the sanctuary and the investigative judgment should be clearly understood by the people of God. All need a knowledge for themselves of the position and work of their great High Priest. Otherwise it will be impossible for them to exercise the faith which is essential at this time or to occupy the position which God designs them to fill. Every individual has a soul to save or to lose. Each has a case pending at the bar of God. Each must meet the great Judge face to face. How important, then, that every mind contemplate often the solemn scene when the judgment shall sit and the books shall be opened, when, with Daniel, every individual must stand in his lot, at the end of the days.

All who have received the light upon these subjects are to bear testimony of the great truths which God has committed to them. The sanctuary in heaven is the very center of Christ's work in behalf of men. It concerns every soul living upon the earth. It opens to view the plan of redemption, bringing us down to the very close of time and revealing the triumphant issue of the contest between righteousness and sin. It is of the utmost importance that all should thoroughly investigate these subjects and be able to give an answer to everyone that asketh them a reason of the hope that is in them.

The intercession of Christ in man's behalf in the sanctuary above is as essential to the plan of salvation as was His death upon the cross. By His death He began that work which after His resurrection He ascended to complete in heaven. We must by faith enter within the veil, "whither the forerunner is for us entered." Hebrews 6:20. There the light from the cross of Calvary is reflected. There we may gain a clearer insight into the mysteries of redemption. The salvation of man is accomplished at an infinite expense to heaven; the sacrifice made is equal to the broadest demands of the broken law of God. Jesus has opened the way to the Father's throne, and through His mediation the sincere desire of all who come to Him in faith may be presented before God.

"He that covereth his sins shall not prosper: but whoso confesseth and forsaketh them shall have mercy." Proverbs 28:13. If those who hide and excuse their faults could see how Satan exults over them, how he taunts Christ and holy angels with their course, they would make haste to confess their sins and to put them away. Through defects in the character, Satan works to gain control of the whole mind, and he knows that if these defects are cherished, he will succeed. Therefore he is constantly seeking to deceive the followers of Christ with his fatal sophistry that it is impossible for them to overcome. But Jesus pleads in their behalf His wounded hands, His bruised body; and He declares to all who would follow Him: "My grace is sufficient for thee." 2 Corinthians 12:9. "Take My yoke upon you, and learn of Me; for I am meek and lowly in heart: and ye shall find rest unto your souls. For My yoke is easy, and My burden is light." Matthew 11:29, 30. Let none, then, regard their defects as incurable. God will give faith and grace to overcome them.

We are now living in the great day of atonement. In the typical service, while the high priest was making the atonement for Israel, all were required to afflict their souls by repentance of sin and humiliation before the Lord, lest they be cut off from among the people. In like manner, all who would have their names retained in the book of life should now, in the few remaining days of their probation, afflict their souls before God by sorrow for sin and true repentance. There must be deep, faithful searching of heart. The light, frivolous spirit indulged by so many professed Christians must be put away. There is earnest warfare before all who would subdue the evil tendencies that strive for the mastery. The work of preparation is an individual work. We are not saved in groups. The purity and devotion of one will not offset the want of these qualities in another. Though all nations are to pass in judgment before God, yet He will examine the case of each individual with as close and searching scrutiny as if there were not another being upon the earth. Everyone must be tested and found without spot or wrinkle or any such thing.

Solemn are the scenes connected with the closing work of the atonement. Momentous are the interests involved therein. The judgment is now passing in the sanctuary above. For many years this work has been in progress. Soon—none know how soon—it will pass to the cases of the living. In the awful presence of God our lives are to come up in review. At this time above all others it behooves every soul to heed the Saviour's admonition: "Watch and pray: for ye know not when the time is." Mark 13:33. "If therefore thou shalt not watch, I will come on thee as a thief, and thou shalt not know what hour I will come upon thee." Revelation 3:3.

When the work of the investigative judgment closes, the destiny of all will have been decided for life or death. Probation is ended a short time before the appearing of the Lord in the clouds of heaven. Christ in the Revelation, looking forward to that time, declares: "He that is unjust, let him be unjust still: and he which is filthy, let him be filthy still: and he that is righteous let him be righteous still: and he that is holy, let him be holy still. And, behold, I come quickly; and My reward is with Me, to give every man according as his work shall be." Revelation 22:11, 12.

The righteous and the wicked will still be living upon the earth in their mortal state—men will be planting and building, eating and drinking, all unconscious that the final, irrevocable decision has been pronounced in the sanctuary above. Before the Flood, after Noah entered the ark, God shut him in and shut the ungodly out; but for seven days the people, knowing not that their doom was fixed, continued their careless, pleasure-loving life and mocked the warnings of impending judgment. "So," says the Saviour, "shall also the coming of the Son of man be." Matthew 24:39. Silently, unnoticed as the midnight thief, will come the decisive hour which marks the fixing of every man's destiny, the final withdrawal of mercy's offer to guilty men.

"Watch ye therefore: ... lest coming suddenly He find you sleeping." Mark 13:35, 36. Perilous is the condition of those who, growing weary of their watch, turn to the attractions of the world. While the man of business is absorbed in the pursuit of gain, while the pleasure lover is seeking indulgence, while the daughter of fashion is arranging her adornments—it may be in that hour the Judge of all the earth will pronounce the sentence: "Thou art weighed in the balances, and art found wanting." Daniel 5:27.

Seven

—The Time of Trouble—

"At that time shall Michael stand up, the great Prince which standeth for the children of thy people: and there shall be a time of trouble, such as never was since there was a nation even to that same time: and at that time thy people shall be delivered, everyone that shall be found written in the book." Daniel 12:1.

When the third angel's message closes, mercy no longer pleads for the guilty inhabitants of the earth. The people of God have accomplished their work. They have received "the latter rain," "the refreshing from the presence of the Lord," and they are prepared for the trying hour before them. Angels are hastening to and fro in heaven. An angel returning from the earth announces that his work is done; the final test has been brought upon the world, and all who have proved themselves loyal to the divine precepts have received "the seal of the living God." Then Jesus ceases His intercession in the sanctuary above. He lifts His hands and with a loud voice says, "It is done;" and all the angelic host lay off their crowns as He makes the solemn announcement: "He that is unjust, let him be unjust still: and he which is filthy, let him be filthy still: and he that is righteous, let him be righteous still: and he that is holy, let him be holy still." Revelation 22:11. Every case has been decided for life or death. Christ has made the atonement for His people and blotted out their sins. The number of His subjects is made up; "the kingdom and dominion, and the greatness of the kingdom under the whole heaven," is about to be given to the heirs of salvation, and Jesus is to reign as King of kings and Lord of lords.

When He leaves the sanctuary, darkness covers the inhabitants of the earth. In that fearful time the righteous must live in the sight of a holy God without an intercessor. The restraint which has been upon the wicked is removed, and Satan has entire control of the finally impenitent. God's long-suffering has ended. The world has rejected His mercy, despised His love, and trampled upon His law. The wicked have passed the boundary of their probation; the Spirit of God, persistently resisted, has been at last withdrawn. Unsheltered by divine grace, they have no protection from the wicked one. Satan will then plunge the inhabitants of the earth into one great, final trouble. As the angels of God cease to hold in check the fierce winds of human passion, all the elements of strife will be let loose. The whole world will be involved in ruin more terrible than that which came upon Jerusalem of old.

A single angel destroyed all the first-born of the Egyptians and filled the land with mourning. When David offended against God by numbering the people, one angel caused that terrible destruction by which his sin was punished. The same destructive power exercised by holy angels when God commands, will be exercised by evil angels when He permits. There are forces now ready, and only waiting the divine permission, to spread desolation everywhere.

Those who honor the law of God have been accused of bringing judgments upon the world, and they will be regarded as the cause of the fearful convulsions of nature and the strife and bloodshed among men that are filling the earth with woe. The power attending the last warning has enraged the wicked; their anger is kindled against all who have received the message, and Satan will excite to still greater intensity the spirit of hatred and persecution.

When God's presence was finally withdrawn from the Jewish nation, priests and people knew it not. Though under the control of Satan, and swayed by the most horrible and malignant passions, they still regarded themselves as the chosen of God. The ministration in the temple continued; sacrifices were offered upon its polluted altars, and daily the divine blessing was invoked upon a people guilty of the blood of God's dear Son and seeking to slay His ministers and apostles. So when the irrevocable decision of the sanctuary has been pronounced and the destiny of the world has been forever fixed, the inhabitants of the earth will know it not. The forms of religion will be continued by a people from whom the Spirit of God has been finally withdrawn; and the satanic zeal with which the prince of evil will inspire them for the accomplishment of his malignant designs, will bear the semblance of zeal for God.

As the Sabbath has become the special point of controversy throughout Christendom, and religious and secular authorities have combined to enforce the observance of the Sunday, the persistent refusal of a small minority to yield to the popular demand will make them objects of universal execration. It will be urged that the few who stand in opposition to an institution of the church and a law of the state ought not to be tolerated; that it is better for them to suffer than for whole nations to be thrown into confusion and lawlessness. The same argument eighteen hundred years ago was brought against Christ by the "rulers of the people." "It is expedient for us," said the wily Caiaphas, "that one man should die for the people, and that the whole nation perish not." John 11:50. This argument will appear conclusive; and a decree will finally be issued against those who hallow the Sabbath of the fourth commandment, denouncing them as deserving of the severest punishment and giving the people liberty, after a certain time, to put them to death. Romanism in the Old World and apostate Protestantism in the New will pursue a similar course toward those who honor all the divine precepts.

The people of God will then be plunged into those scenes of affliction and distress described by the prophet as the time of Jacob's trouble. "Thus saith the Lord: We have heard a voice of trembling, of fear, and not of peace. ... All faces are turned into paleness. Alas! for that day is great, so that none is like it: it is even the time of Jacob's trouble; but he shall be saved out of it." Jeremiah 30:5-7.

Jacob's night of anguish, when he wrestled in prayer for deliverance from the hand of Esau (Genesis 32:24-30), represents the experience of God's people in the time of trouble. Because of the deception practiced to secure his father's blessing, intended for Esau, Jacob had fled for his life, alarmed by his brother's deadly threats. After remaining for many years an exile, he had set out, at God's command, to return with his wives and children, his flocks and herds, to his native country. On reaching the borders of the land, he was filled with terror by the tidings of Esau's approach at the head of a band of warriors, doubtless bent upon revenge. Jacob's company, unarmed and defenseless, seemed about to fall helpless victims of violence and slaughter. And to the burden of anxiety and fear was added the crushing weight of self-reproach, for it was his own sin that had brought this danger. His only hope was in the mercy of God; his only defense must be prayer.

Yet he leaves nothing undone on his own part to atone for the wrong to his brother and to avert the threatened danger. So should the followers of Christ, as they approach the time of trouble, make every exertion to place themselves in a proper light before the people, to disarm prejudice, and to avert the danger which threatens liberty of conscience.

Having sent his family away, that they may not witness his distress, Jacob remains alone to intercede with God. He confesses his sin and gratefully acknowledges the mercy of God toward him while with deep humiliation he pleads the covenant made with his fathers and the promises to himself in the night vision at Bethel and in the land of his exile. The crisis in his life has come; everything is at stake. In the darkness and solitude he continues praying and humbling himself before God. Suddenly a hand is laid upon his shoulder. He thinks that an enemy is seeking his life, and with all the energy of despair he wrestles with his assailant. As the day begins to break, the stranger puts forth his superhuman power; at his touch the strong man seems paralyzed, and he falls, a helpless, weeping suppliant, upon the neck of his mysterious antagonist. Jacob knows now that it is the Angel of the covenant with whom he has been in conflict. Though disabled and suffering the keenest pain, he does not relinquish his purpose. Long has he endured perplexity, remorse, and trouble for his sin; now he must have the assurance that it is pardoned. The divine visitant seems about to depart; but Jacob clings to Him, pleading for a blessing. The Angel urges, "Let Me go, for the day breaketh;" but the patriarch exclaims, "I will not let Thee go, except Thou bless me." What confidence, what firmness and perseverance, are here displayed! Had this been a boastful, presumptuous claim, Jacob would have been instantly destroyed; but his was the assurance of one who confesses his weakness and unworthiness, yet trusts the mercy of a covenant-keeping God.

"He had power over the Angel, and prevailed." Hosea 12:4. Through humiliation, repentance, and self-surrender, this sinful, erring mortal prevailed with the Majesty of heaven. He had fastened his trembling grasp upon the promises of God, and the heart of Infinite Love could not turn away the sinner's plea. As an evidence of his triumph and an encouragement to others to imitate his example, his name was changed from one which was a reminder of his sin, to one that commemorated his victory. And the fact that Jacob had prevailed with God was an assurance that he would prevail with men. He no longer feared to encounter his brother's anger, for the Lord was his defense.

Satan had accused Jacob before the angels of God, claiming the right to destroy him because of his sin; he had moved upon Esau to march against him; and during the patriarch's long night of wrestling, Satan endeavored to force upon him a sense of his guilt in order to discourage him and break his hold upon God. Jacob was driven almost to despair; but he knew that without help from heaven he must perish. He had sincerely repented of his great sin, and he appealed to the mercy of God. He would not be turned from his purpose, but held fast the Angel and urged his petition with earnest, agonizing cries until he prevailed.

As Satan influenced Esau to march against Jacob, so he will stir up the wicked to destroy God's people in the time of trouble. And as he accused Jacob, he will urge his accusations against the people of God. He numbers the world as his subjects; but the little company who keep the commandments of God are resisting his supremacy. If he could blot them from the earth, his triumph would be complete. He sees that holy angels are guarding them, and he infers that their sins have been pardoned; but he does not know that their cases have been decided in the sanctuary above. He has an accurate knowledge of the sins which he has tempted them to commit, and he presents these before God in the most exaggerated light, representing this people to be just as deserving as himself of exclusion from the favor of God. He declares that the Lord cannot in justice forgive their sins and yet destroy him and his angels. He claims them as his prey and demands that they be given into his hands to destroy.

As Satan accuses the people of God on account of their sins, the Lord permits him to try them to the uttermost. Their confidence in God, their faith and firmness, will be severely tested. As they review the past, their hopes sink; for in their whole lives they can see little good. They are fully conscious of their weakness and unworthiness. Satan endeavors to terrify them with the thought that their cases are hopeless, that the stain of their defilement will never be washed away. He hopes so to destroy their faith that they will yield to his temptations and turn from their allegiance to God.

Though God's people will be surrounded by enemies who are bent upon their destruction, yet the anguish which they suffer is not a dread of persecution for the truth's sake; they fear that every sin has not been repented of, and that through some fault in themselves they will fail to realize the fulfillment of the Saviour's promise: I "will keep thee from the hour of temptation, which shall come upon all the world." Revelation 3:10. If they could have the assurance of pardon they would not shrink from torture or death; but should they prove unworthy, and lose their lives because of their own defects of character, then God's holy name would be reproached.

On every hand they hear the plottings of treason and see the active working of rebellion; and there is aroused within them an intense desire, an earnest yearning of soul, that this great apostasy may be terminated and the wickedness of the wicked may come to an end. But while they plead with God to stay the work of rebellion, it is with a keen sense of self-reproach that they themselves have no more power to resist and urge back the mighty tide of evil. They feel that had they always employed all their ability in the service of Christ, going forward from strength to strength, Satan's forces would have less power to prevail against them.

They afflict their souls before God, pointing to their past repentance of their many sins, and pleading the Saviour's promise: "Let him take hold of My strength, that he may make peace with Me; and he shall make peace with Me." Isaiah 27:5. Their faith does not fail because their prayers are not immediately answered. Though suffering the keenest anxiety, terror, and distress, they do not cease their intercessions. They lay hold of the strength of God as Jacob laid hold of the Angel; and the language of their souls is: "I will not let Thee go, except Thou bless me."

Had not Jacob previously repented of his sin in obtaining the birthright by fraud, God would not have heard his prayer and mercifully preserved his life. So, in the time of trouble, if the people of God had unconfessed sins to appear before them while tortured with fear and anguish, they would be overwhelmed; despair would cut off their faith, and they could not have confidence to plead with God for deliverance. But while they have a deep sense of their unworthiness, they have no concealed wrongs to reveal. Their sins have gone beforehand to judgment and have been blotted out, and they cannot bring them to remembrance.

Satan leads many to believe that God will overlook their unfaithfulness in the minor affairs of life; but the Lord shows in His dealings with Jacob that He will in no wise sanction or tolerate evil. All who endeavor to excuse or conceal their sins, and permit them to remain upon the books of heaven, unconfessed and unforgiven, will be overcome by Satan. The more exalted their profession and the more honorable the position which they hold, the more grievous is their course in the sight of God and the more sure the triumph of their great adversary. Those who delay a preparation for the day of God cannot obtain it in the time of trouble or at any subsequent time. The case of all such is hopeless.

Those professed Christians who come up to that last fearful conflict unprepared will, in their despair, confess their sins in words of burning anguish, while the wicked exult over their distress. These confessions are of the same character as was that of Esau or of Judas. Those who make them, lament the *result* of transgression, but not its guilt. They feel no true contrition, no abhorrence of evil. They acknowledge their sin, through fear of punishment; but, like Pharaoh of old, they would return to their defiance of Heaven should the judgments be removed.

Jacob's history is also an assurance that God will not cast off those who have been deceived and tempted and betrayed into sin, but who have returned unto Him with true repentance. While Satan seeks to destroy this class, God will send His angels to comfort and protect them in the time of peril. The assaults of Satan are fierce and determined, his delusions are terrible; but the Lord's eye is upon His people, and His ear listens to their cries. Their affliction is great, the flames of the furnace seem about to consume them; but the Refiner will bring them forth as gold tried in the fire. God's love for His children during the period of their severest trial is as strong and tender as in the days of their sunniest prosperity; but it is needful for them to be placed in the furnace of fire; their earthliness must be consumed, that the image of Christ may be perfectly reflected.

The season of distress and anguish before us will require a faith that can endure weariness, delay, and hunger—a faith that will not faint though severely tried. The period of probation is granted to all to prepare for that time. Jacob prevailed because he was persevering and determined. His victory is an evidence of the power of importunate prayer. All who will lay hold of God's promises, as he did, and be as earnest and persevering as he was, will succeed as he succeeded. Those who are unwilling to deny self, to agonize before God, to pray long and earnestly for His blessing, will not obtain it. Wrestling with God—how few know what it is! How few have ever had their souls drawn out after God with intensity of desire until every power is on the stretch. When waves of despair which no language can express sweep over the suppliant, how few cling with unyielding faith to the promises of God.

Those who exercise but little faith now, are in the greatest danger of falling under the power of satanic delusions and the decree to compel the conscience. And even if they endure the test they will be plunged into deeper distress and anguish in the time of trouble, because they have never made it a habit to trust in God. The lessons of faith which they have neglected they will be forced to learn under a terrible pressure of discouragement.

We should now acquaint ourselves with God by proving His promises. Angels record every prayer that is earnest and sincere. We should rather dispense with selfish gratifications than neglect communion with God. The deepest poverty, the greatest self-denial, with His approval, is better than riches, honors, ease, and friendship without it. We must take time to pray. If we allow our minds to be absorbed by worldly interests, the Lord may give us time by removing from us our idols of gold, of houses, or of fertile lands.

The young would not be seduced into sin if they would refuse to enter any path save that upon which they could ask God's blessing. If the messengers who bear the last solemn warning to the world would pray for the blessing of God, not in a cold, listless, lazy manner, but fervently and in faith, as did Jacob, they would find many places where they could say: "I have seen God face to face, and my life is preserved." Genesis 32:30. They would be accounted of heaven as princes, having power to prevail with God and with men.

The "time of trouble, such as never was," is soon to open upon us; and we shall need an experience which we do not now possess and which many are too indolent to obtain. It is often the case that trouble is greater in anticipation than in reality; but this is not true of the crisis before us. The most vivid presentation cannot reach the magnitude of the ordeal. In that time of trial, every soul must stand for himself before God. "Though Noah, Daniel, and Job" were in the land, "as I live, saith the Lord God, they shall deliver neither son nor daughter; they shall but deliver their own souls by their righteousness." Ezekiel 14:20.

Now, while our great High Priest is making the atonement for us, we should seek to become perfect in Christ. Not even by a thought could our Saviour be brought to yield to the power of temptation. Satan finds in human hearts some point where he can gain a foothold; some sinful desire is cherished, by means of which his temptations assert their power. But Christ declared of Himself: "The prince of this world cometh, and hath nothing in Me." John 14:30. Satan could find nothing in the Son of God that would enable him to gain the victory. He had kept His Father's commandments, and there was no sin in Him that Satan could use to his advantage. This is the condition in which those must be found who shall stand in the time of trouble.

It is in this life that we are to separate sin from us, through faith in the atoning blood of Christ. Our precious Saviour invites us to join ourselves to Him, to unite our weakness to His strength, our ignorance to His wisdom, our unworthiness to His merits. God's providence is the school in which we are to learn the meekness and lowliness of Jesus. The Lord is ever setting before us, not the way we would choose, which seems easier and pleasanter to us, but the true aims of life. It rests with us to co-operate with the agencies which Heaven employs in the work of conforming our characters to the divine model. None can neglect or defer this work but at the most fearful peril to their souls.

The apostle John in vision heard a loud voice in heaven exclaiming: "Woe to the inhabiters of the earth and of the sea! for the devil is come down unto you, having great wrath, because he knoweth that he hath but a short time." Revelation 12:12. Fearful are the scenes which call forth this exclamation from the heavenly voice. The wrath of Satan increases as his time grows short, and his work of deceit and destruction will reach its culmination in the time of trouble.

Fearful sights of a supernatural character will soon be revealed in the heavens, in token of the power of miracle-working demons. The spirits of devils will go forth to the kings of the earth and to the whole world, to fasten them in deception, and urge them on to unite with Satan in his last struggle against the government of heaven. By these agencies, rulers and subjects will be alike deceived. Persons will arise pretending to be Christ Himself, and claiming the title and worship which belong to the world's Redeemer. They will perform wonderful miracles of healing and will profess to have revelations from heaven contradicting the testimony of the Scriptures.

As the crowning act in the great drama of deception, Satan himself will personate Christ. The church has long professed to look to the

Saviour's advent as the consummation of her hopes. Now the great deceiver will make it appear that Christ has come. In different parts of the earth, Satan will manifest himself among men as a majestic being of dazzling brightness, resembling the description of the Son of God given by John in the Revelation. Revelation 1:13-15. The glory that surrounds him is unsurpassed by anything that mortal eyes have yet beheld. The shout of triumph rings out upon the air: "Christ has come! Christ has come!" The people prostrate themselves in adoration before him, while he lifts up his hands and pronounces a blessing upon them, as Christ blessed His disciples when He was upon the earth. His voice is soft and subdued, yet full of melody. In gentle, compassionate tones he presents some of the same gracious, heavenly truths which the Saviour uttered; he heals the diseases of the people, and then, in his assumed character of Christ, he claims to have changed the Sabbath to Sunday, and commands all to hallow the day which he has blessed. He declares that those who persist in keeping holy the seventh day are blaspheming his name by refusing to listen to his angels sent to them with light and truth. This is the strong, almost overmastering delusion. Like the Samaritans who were deceived by Simon Magus, the multitudes, from the least to the greatest, give heed to these sorceries, saying: This is "the great power of God." Acts 8:10.

But the people of God will not be misled. The teachings of this false christ are not in accordance with the Scriptures. His blessing is pronounced upon the worshipers of the beast and his image, the very class upon whom the Bible declares that God's unmingled wrath shall be poured out.

And, furthermore, Satan is not permitted to counterfeit the manner of Christ's advent. The Saviour has warned His people against deception upon this point, and has clearly foretold the manner of His second coming. "There shall arise false christs, and false prophets, and shall show great signs and wonders; insomuch that, if it were possible, they shall deceive the very elect. ... Wherefore if they shall say unto you, Behold, He is in the desert; go not forth; behold, He is in the secret chambers; believe it not. For as the lightning cometh out of the east, and shineth even unto the west; so shall also the coming of the Son of man be." Matthew 24:24-27, 31; 25:31; Revelation 1:7; 1 Thessalonians 4:16, 17. This coming there is no possibility of counterfeiting. It will be universally known—witnessed by the whole world.

Only those who have been diligent students of the Scriptures and who have received the love of the truth will be shielded from the powerful delusion that takes the world captive. By the Bible testimony these will detect the deceiver in his disguise. To all the testing time will come. By the sifting of temptation the genuine Christian will be revealed. Are the people of God now so firmly established upon His word that they would not yield to the evidence of their senses? Would they, in such a crisis, cling to the Bible and the Bible only? Satan will, if possible, prevent them from obtaining a preparation to stand in that day. He will so arrange affairs as to hedge up their way, entangle them with earthly treasures, cause them to carry a heavy, wearisome burden, that their hearts may be overcharged with the cares of this life and the day of trial may come upon them as a thief.

As the decree issued by the various rulers of Christendom against commandment keepers shall withdraw the protection of government and abandon them to those who desire their destruction, the people of God will flee from the cities and villages and associate together in companies, dwelling in the most desolate and solitary places. Many will find refuge in the strongholds of the mountains. Like the Christians of the Piedmont valleys, they will make the high places of the earth their sanctuaries and will thank God for "the munitions of rocks." Isaiah 33:16. But many of all nations and of all classes, high and low, rich and poor, black and white, will be cast into the most unjust and cruel bondage. The beloved of God pass weary days, bound in chains, shut in by prison bars, sentenced to be slain, some apparently left to die of starvation in dark and loathsome dungeons. No human ear is open to hear their moans; no human hand is ready to lend them help.

Will the Lord forget His people in this trying hour? Did He forget faithful Noah when judgments were visited upon the antediluvian world? Did He forget Lot when the fire came down from heaven to consume the cities of the plain? Did He forget Joseph surrounded by idolaters in Egypt? Did He forget Elijah when the oath of Jezebel threatened him with the fate of the prophets of Baal? Did He forget Jeremiah in the dark and dismal pit of his prison house? Did He forget the three worthies in the fiery furnace? or Daniel in the den of lions?

"Zion said, The Lord hath forsaken me, and my Lord hath forgotten me. Can a woman forget her sucking child, that she should not have compassion on the son of her womb? yea, they may forget, yet will I not forget thee. Behold, I have graven thee upon the palms of My hands." Isaiah 49:14-16. The Lord of hosts has said: "He that toucheth you toucheth the apple of His eye." Zechariah 2:8.

Though enemies may thrust them into prison, yet dungeon walls cannot cut off the communication between their souls and Christ. One who sees their every weakness, who is acquainted with every trial, is above all earthly powers; and angels will come to them in lonely cells, bringing light and peace from heaven. The prison will be as a palace; for the rich in faith dwell there, and the gloomy walls will be lighted up with heavenly light as when Paul and Silas prayed and sang praises at midnight in the Philippian dungeon.

God's judgments will be visited upon those who are seeking to oppress and destroy His people. His long forbearance with the wicked emboldens men in transgression, but their punishment is nonetheless certain and terrible because it is long delayed. "The Lord shall rise up as in Mount Perazim, He shall be wroth as in the valley of Gibeon, that He may do His work, His strange work; and bring to pass His act, His strange act." Isaiah 28:21. To our merciful God the act of punishment is a strange act. "As I live, saith the Lord God, I have no pleasure in the death of the wicked." Ezekiel 33:11. The Lord is "merciful and gracious, long-suffering, and abundant in goodness and truth, ... forgiving iniquity and transgression and sin." Yet He will "by no means clear the guilty." The Lord is slow to anger, and great in power, and will not at all acquit the wicked." Exodus 34:6, 7; Nahum 1:3. By terrible things in righteousness He will vindicate the authority of His downtrodden law. The severity of the retribution awaiting the transgressor may be judged by the Lord's reluctance to execute justice. The nation with which He bears long, and which He will not smite until it has filled up the measure of its iniquity in God's account, will finally drink the cup of wrath unmixed with mercy.

When Christ ceases His intercession in the sanctuary, the unmingled wrath threatened against those who worship the beast and his image and receive his mark (Revelation 14:9, 10), will be poured out. The plagues upon Egypt when God was about to deliver Israel were similar in character to those more terrible and extensive judgments which are to fall upon the world just before the final deliverance of God's people. Says the revelator, in describing those terrific scourges: "There fell a noisome and grievous sore upon the men which had the mark of the beast, and upon them which worshiped his image." The sea "became as the blood of a dead man: and every living soul died in the sea." And "the rivers and fountains of waters ... became blood." Terrible as these inflictions are, God's justice stands fully vindicated. The angel of God declares: "Thou art righteous, O Lord, ... because Thou hast judged thus. For they have shed the blood of saints and prophets, and Thou hast given them blood to drink; for they are worthy." Revelation 16:2-6. By condemning the people of God to death, they have as truly incurred the guilt of their blood as if it had been shed by their hands. In like manner Christ declared the Jews of His time guilty of all the blood of holy men which had been shed since the days of Abel; for they possessed the same spirit and were seeking to do the same work with these murderers of the prophets.

In the plague that follows, power is given to the sun "to scorch men with fire. And men were scorched with great heat." Verses 8, 9. The prophets thus describe the condition of the earth at this fearful time: "The land mourneth; ... because the harvest of the field is perished. ... All the trees of the field are withered: because joy is withered away from the sons of men." "The seed is rotten under their clods, the garners are laid desolate. ... How do the beasts groan! the herds of cattle are perplexed, because they have no pasture. ... The rivers of water are dried up, and the fire hath devoured the pastures of the wilderness." "The songs of the temple shall be howlings in that day, saith the Lord God: there shall be many dead bodies in every place; they shall cast them forth with silence." Joel 1:10-12, 17-20; Amos 8:3.

These plagues are not universal, or the inhabitants of the earth would be wholly cut off. Yet they will be the most awful scourges that have ever been known to mortals. All the judgments upon men, prior to the close of probation, have been mingled with mercy. The pleading blood of Christ has shielded the sinner from receiving the full measure of his guilt; but in the final judgment, wrath is poured out unmixed with mercy.

In that day, multitudes will desire the shelter of God's mercy which they have so long despised. "Behold, the days come, saith the Lord God, that I will send a famine in the land, not a famine of bread, nor a thirst for water, but of hearing the words of the Lord: and they shall wander from sea to sea, and from the north even to the east, they shall run to and fro to seek the word of the Lord, and shall not find it." Amos 8:11, 12.

The people of God will not be free from suffering; but while persecuted and distressed, while they endure privation and suffer for want of food they will not be left to perish. That God who cared for Elijah will not pass by one of His self-sacrificing children. He who numbers the hairs of their head will care for them, and in time of famine they shall be satisfied. While the wicked are dying from hunger and pestilence, angels will shield the righteous and supply their wants. To him that "walketh righteously" is the promise: "Bread shall be given him; his waters shall be sure." "When the poor and needy seek water, and there is none, and their tongue faileth for thirst, I the Lord will hear them, I the God of Israel will not forsake them." Isaiah 33:15, 16; 41:17.

"Although the fig tree shall not blossom, neither shall fruit be in the vines; the labor of the olive shall fail, and the fields shall yield no meat; the flock shall be cut off from the fold, and there shall be no herd in the stalls;" yet shall they that fear Him "rejoice in the Lord" and joy in the God of their salvation. Habakkuk 3:17, 18.

"The Lord is thy keeper: the Lord is thy shade upon thy right hand. The sun shall not smite thee by day, nor the moon by night. The Lord shall preserve thee from all evil: He shall preserve thy soul." "He shall deliver thee from the snare of the fowler, and from the noisome pestilence. He shall cover thee with His feathers, and under His wings shalt thou trust: His truth shall be thy shield and buckler. Thou shalt not be afraid for the terror by night; nor for the arrow that flieth by day; nor for the pestilence that walketh in darkness; nor for the destruction that wasteth at noonday. A thousand shall fall at thy side, and ten thousand at thy right hand; but it shall not come nigh thee. Only with thine eyes shalt thou behold and see the reward of the wicked. Because thou hast made the Lord, which is my refuge, even the Most High, thy habitation; there shall no evil befall thee, neither shall any plague come nigh thy dwelling." Psalms 121:5-7; 91:3-10.

Yet to human sight it will appear that the people of God must soon seal their testimony with their blood as did the martyrs before them. They themselves begin to fear that the Lord has left them to fall by the hand of their enemies. It is a time of fearful agony. Day and night they cry unto God for deliverance. The wicked exult, and the jeering cry is heard: "Where now is your faith? Why does not God deliver you out of our hands if you are indeed His people?" But the waiting ones remember Jesus dying upon Calvary's cross and the chief priests and rulers shouting in mockery: "He saved others; Himself He cannot save. If He be the King of Israel, let Him now come down from the cross, and we will believe Him." Matthew 27:42. Like Jacob, all are wrestling with God. Their countenances express their internal struggle. Paleness sits upon every face. Yet they cease not their earnest intercession.

Could men see with heavenly vision, they would behold companies of angels that excel in strength stationed about those who have kept the word of Christ's patience. With sympathizing tenderness, angels have witnessed their distress and have heard their prayers. They are waiting the word of their Commander to snatch them from their peril. But they must wait yet a little longer. The people of God must drink of the cup and be baptized with the baptism. The very delay, so painful to them, is the best answer to their petitions. As they endeavor to wait trustingly for the Lord to work they are led to exercise faith, hope, and patience, which have been too little exercised during their religious experience. Yet for the elect's sake the time of trouble will be shortened. "Shall not God avenge His own elect, which cry day and night unto Him? ... I tell you that He will avenge them speedily." Luke 18:7, 8. The end will come more quickly than men expect. The wheat will be gathered and bound in sheaves for the garner of God; the tares will be bound as fagots for the fires of destruction.

The heavenly sentinels, faithful to their trust, continue their watch. Though a general decree has fixed the time when commandment keepers may be put to death, their enemies will in some cases anticipate the decree, and before the time specified, will endeavor to take their lives. But none can pass the mighty guardians stationed about every faithful soul. Some are assailed in their flight from the cities and villages; but the swords raised against them break and fall powerless as a straw. Others are defended by angels in the form of men of war.

In all ages, God has wrought through holy angels for the succor and deliverance of His people. Celestial beings have taken an active part in the affairs of men. They have appeared clothed in garments that shone as the lightning; they have come as men in the garb of wayfarers. Angels have appeared in human form to men of God. They have rested, as if weary, under the oaks at noon. They have accepted the hospitalities of human homes. They have acted as guides to benighted travelers. They have, with their own hands, kindled the fires at the altar. They have opened prison doors and set free the servants of the Lord. Clothed with the panoply of heaven, they came to roll away the stone from the Saviour's tomb.

In the form of men, angels are often in the assemblies of the righteous; and they visit the assemblies of the wicked, as they went to Sodom, to make a record of their deeds, to determine whether they have passed the boundary of God's forbearance. The Lord delights in mercy; and for the sake of a few who really serve Him, He restrains calamities and prolongs the tranquillity of multitudes. Little do sinners against God realize that they are indebted for their own lives to the faithful few whom they delight to ridicule and oppress.

Though the rulers of this world know it not, yet often in their councils angels have been spokesmen. Human eyes have looked upon them; human ears have listened to their appeals; human lips have opposed their suggestions and ridiculed their counsels; human hands have met them with insult and abuse. In the council hall and the court of justice these heavenly messengers have shown an intimate acquaintance with human history; they have proved themselves better able to plead the cause of the oppressed than were their ablest and most eloquent defenders. They have defeated purposes and arrested evils that would have greatly retarded the work of God and would have caused great suffering to His people. In the hour of peril and distress "the angel of the Lord encampeth round about them that fear Him, and delivereth them." Psalm 34:7.

With earnest longing, God's people await the tokens of their coming King. As the watchmen are accosted, "What of the night?" the answer is given unfalteringly, "The morning cometh, and also the night." Isaiah 21:11, 12. Light is gleaming upon the clouds above the mountaintops. Soon there will be a revealing of His glory. The Sun of Righteousness is about to shine forth. The morning and the night are both at hand—the opening of endless day to the righteous, the settling down of eternal night to the wicked."

As the wrestling ones urge their petitions before God, the veil separating them from the unseen seems almost withdrawn. The heavens glow with the dawning of eternal day, and like the melody of angel songs the words fall upon the ear: "Stand fast to your allegiance. Help is coming." Christ, the almighty Victor, holds out to His weary soldiers a crown of immortal glory; and His voice comes from the gates ajar: "Lo, I am with you. Be not afraid. I am acquainted with all your sorrows; I have borne your griefs. You are not warring against untried enemies. I have fought the battle in your behalf, and in My name you are more than conquerors."

The precious Saviour will send help just when we need it. The way to heaven is consecrated by His footprints. Every thorn that wounds our feet has wounded His. Every cross that we are called to bear He has borne before us. The Lord permits conflicts, to prepare the soul for peace. The time of trouble is a fearful ordeal for God's people; but it is the time for every true believer to look up, and by faith he may see the bow of promise encircling him.

"The redeemed of the Lord shall return, and come with singing unto Zion; and everlasting joy shall be upon their head: they shall obtain gladness and joy; and sorrow and mourning shall flee away. I, even I, am He that comforteth you: who art thou, that thou shouldest be afraid of a man that shall die, and of the son of man which shall be made as grass; and forgettest the Lord thy Maker; ... and hast feared continually every day because of the fury of the oppressor, as if he were ready to destroy? and where is the fury of the oppressor? The captive exile hasteneth that he may be loosed, and that he should not die in the pit, nor that his bread should fail. But I am the Lord thy God, that divided the sea, whose waves roared: The Lord of hosts is His name. And I have put My words in thy mouth, and I have covered thee in the shadow of Mine hand." Isaiah 51:11-16.

"Therefore hear now this, thou afflicted, and drunken, but not with wine: Thus saith thy Lord the Lord, and thy God that pleadeth the cause of His people, Behold, I have taken out of thine hand the cup of trembling, even the dregs of the cup of My fury; thou shalt no more drink it again: but I will put it into the hand of them that afflict thee; which have said to thy soul, Bow down, that we may go over: and thou hast laid thy body as the ground, and as the street, to them that went over." Verses 21-23.

The eye of God, looking down the ages, was fixed upon the crisis which His people are to meet, when earthly powers shall be arrayed against them. Like the captive exile, they will be in fear of death by starvation or by violence. But the Holy One who divided the Red Sea before Israel, will manifest His mighty power and turn their captivity.

"They shall be Mine, saith the Lord of hosts, in that day when I make up My jewels; and I will spare them, as a man spareth his own son that serveth him." Malachi 3:17. If the blood of Christ's faithful witnesses were shed at this time, it would not, like the blood of the martyrs, be as seed sown to yield a harvest for God. Their fidelity would not be a testimony to convince others of the truth; for the obdurate heart has beaten back the waves of mercy until they return no more. If the righteous were now left to fall a prey to their enemies, it would be a triumph for the prince of darkness. Says the psalmist: "In the time of trouble He shall hide me in His pavilion: in the secret of His tabernacle shall He hide me." Psalm 27:5. Christ has spoken: "Come, My people, enter thou into thy chambers, and shut thy doors about thee: hide thyself as it were for a little moment, until the indignation be overpast. For, behold, the Lord cometh out of His place to punish the inhabitants of the earth for their iniquity." Isaiah 26:20, 21. Glorious will be the deliverance of those who have patiently waited for His coming and whose names are written in the book of life.

Eight

—God's People Delivered—

When the protection of human laws shall be withdrawn from those who honor the law of God, there will be, in different lands, a simultaneous movement for their destruction. As the time appointed in the decree draws near, the people will conspire to root out the hated sect. It will be determined to strike in one night a decisive blow, which shall utterly silence the voice of dissent and reproof.

The people of God—some in prison cells, some hidden in solitary retreats in the forests and the mountains—still plead for divine protection, while in every quarter companies of armed men, urged on by hosts of evil angels, are preparing for the work of death. It is now, in the hour of utmost extremity, that the God of Israel will interpose for the deliverance of His chosen. Saith the Lord; "Ye shall have a song, as in the night when a holy solemnity is kept; and gladness of heart, as when one goeth … to come into the mountain of the Lord, to the Mighty One of Israel. And the Lord shall cause His glorious voice to be heard, and shall show the lighting down of His arm, with the indignation of His anger, and with the flame of a devouring fire, with scattering, and tempest, and hailstones." Isaiah 30:29, 30.

With shouts of triumph, jeering, and imprecation, throngs of evil men are about to rush upon their prey, when, lo, a dense blackness, deeper than the darkness of the night, falls upon the earth. Then a rainbow, shining with the glory from the throne of God, spans the heavens and seems to encircle each praying company. The angry multitudes are suddenly arrested. Their mocking cries die away. The objects of their murderous rage are forgotten. With fearful forebodings they gaze upon the symbol of God's covenant and long to be shielded from its overpowering brightness.

By the people of God a voice, clear and melodious, is heard, saying, "Look up," and lifting their eyes to the heavens, they behold the bow of promise. The black, angry clouds that covered the firmament are parted, and like Stephen they look up steadfastly into heaven and see the glory of God and the Son of man seated upon His throne. In His divine form they discern the marks of His humiliation; and from His lips they hear the request presented before His Father and the holy angels: "I will that they also, whom Thou hast given Me, be with Me where I am." John 17:24. Again a voice, musical and triumphant, is heard, saying: "They come! they come! holy, harmless, and undefiled. They have kept the word of My patience; they shall walk among the angels;" and the pale, quivering lips of those who have held fast their faith utter a shout of victory.

It is at midnight that God manifests His power for the deliverance of His people. The sun appears, shining in its strength. Signs and wonders follow in quick succession. The wicked look with terror and amazement upon the scene, while the righteous behold with solemn joy the tokens of their deliverance. Everything in nature seems turned out of its course. The streams cease to flow. Dark, heavy clouds come up and clash against each other. In the midst of the angry heavens is one clear space of indescribable glory, whence comes the voice of God like the sound of many waters, saying: "It is done." Revelation 16:17.

That voice shakes the heavens and the earth. There is a mighty earthquake, "such as was not since men were upon the earth, so mighty an earthquake, and so great." Verses 17, 18. The firmament appears to open and shut. The glory from the throne of God seems flashing through. The mountains shake like a reed in the wind, and ragged rocks are scattered on every side. There is a roar as of a coming tempest. The sea is lashed into fury. There is heard the shriek of a hurricane like the voice of demons upon a mission of destruction. The whole earth heaves and swells like the waves of the sea. Its surface is breaking up. Its very foundations seem to be giving way. Mountain chains are sinking. Inhabited islands disappear. The seaports that have become like Sodom for wickedness are swallowed up by the angry waters. Babylon the great has come in remembrance before God, "to give unto her the cup of the wine of the fierceness of His wrath." Great hailstones, every one "about the weight of a talent," are doing their work of destruction. Verses 19, 21. The proudest cities of the earth are laid low. The lordly palaces, upon which the world's great men have lavished their wealth in order to glorify themselves, are crumbling to ruin before their eyes. Prison walls are rent asunder, and God's people, who have been held in bondage for their faith, are set free.

Graves are opened, and "many of them that sleep in the dust of the earth. ... awake, some to everlasting life, and some to shame and everlasting contempt." Daniel 12:2. All who have died in the faith of the third angel's message come forth from the tomb glorified, to hear God's covenant of peace with those who have kept His law. "They also which pierced Him" (Revelation 1:7), those that mocked and derided Christ's dying agonies, and the most violent opposers of His truth and His people, are raised to behold Him in His glory and to see the honor placed upon the loyal and obedient.

Thick clouds still cover the sky; yet the sun now and then breaks through, appearing like the avenging eye of Jehovah. Fierce lightnings leap from the heavens, enveloping the earth in a sheet of flame. Above the terrific roar of thunder, voices, mysterious and awful, declare the doom of the wicked. The words spoken are not comprehended by all; but they are distinctly understood by the false teachers. Those who a little before were so reckless, so boastful and defiant, so exultant in their cruelty to God's commandment-keeping people, are now overwhelmed with consternation and shuddering in fear. Their wails are heard above the sound of the elements. Demons acknowledge the deity of Christ and tremble before His power, while men are supplicating for mercy and groveling in abject terror.

Said the prophets of old, as they beheld in holy vision the day of God: "Howl ye; for the day of the Lord is at hand; it shall come as a destruction from the Almighty." Isaiah 13:6. "Enter into the rock, and hide thee in the dust, for fear of the Lord, and for the glory of His majesty. The lofty looks of man shall be humbled, and the haughtiness of men shall be bowed down, and the Lord alone shall be exalted in that day. For the day of the Lord of hosts shall be upon everyone that is proud and lofty, and upon everyone that is lifted up; and he shall be brought low." "In that day a man shall cast the idols of his silver, and the idols of his gold, which they made each one for himself to worship, to the moles and to the bats; to go into the clefts of the rocks, and into the tops of the ragged rocks, for fear of the Lord, and for the glory of His majesty, when He ariseth to shake terribly the earth." Isaiah 2:10-12, 20, 21, margin.

Through a rift in the clouds there beams a star whose brilliancy is increased fourfold in contrast with the darkness. It speaks hope and joy to the faithful, but severity and wrath to the transgressors of God's law. Those who have sacrificed all for Christ are now secure, hidden as in the secret of the Lord's pavilion. They have been tested, and before the world and the despisers of truth they have evinced their fidelity to Him who died for them. A marvelous change has come over those who have held fast their integrity in the very face of death. They have been suddenly delivered from the dark and terrible tyranny of men transformed to demons. Their faces, so lately pale, anxious, and haggard, are now aglow with wonder, faith, and love. Their voices rise in triumphant song: "God is our refuge and strength, a very present help in trouble. Therefore will not we fear, though the earth be removed, and though the mountains be carried into the midst of the sea; though the waters thereof roar and be troubled, though the mountains shake with the swelling thereof." Psalm 46:1-3.

While these words of holy trust ascend to God, the clouds sweep back, and the starry heavens are seen, unspeakably glorious in contrast with the black and angry firmament on either side. The glory of the celestial city streams from the gates ajar. Then there appears against the sky a hand holding two tables of stone folded together. Says the prophet: "The heavens shall declare His righteousness: for God is judge Himself." Psalm 50:6. That holy law, God's righteousness, that amid thunder and flame was proclaimed from Sinai as the guide of life, is now revealed to men as the rule of judgment. The hand opens the tables, and there are seen the precepts of the Decalogue, traced as with a pen of fire. The words are so plain that all can read them. Memory is aroused, the darkness of superstition and heresy is swept from every mind, and God's ten words, brief, comprehensive, and authoritative, are presented to the view of all the inhabitants of the earth.

It is impossible to describe the horror and despair of those who have trampled upon God's holy requirements. The Lord gave them His law; they might have compared their characters with it and learned their defects while there was yet opportunity for repentance and reform; but in order to secure the favor of the world, they set aside its precepts and taught others to transgress. They have endeavored to compel God's people to profane His Sabbath. Now they are condemned by that law which they have despised. With awful distinctness they see that they are without excuse. They chose whom they would serve and worship. "Then shall ye return, and discern between the righteous and the wicked, between him that serveth God and him that serveth Him not." Malachi 3:18.

The enemies of God's law, from the ministers down to the least among them, have a new conception of truth and duty. Too late they see that the Sabbath of the fourth commandment is the seal of the living God. Too late they see the true nature of their spurious sabbath and the sandy foundation upon which they have been building. They find that they have been fighting against God. Religious teachers have led souls to perdition while professing to guide them to the gates of Paradise. Not until the day of final accounts will it be known how great is the responsibility of men in holy office and how terrible are the results of their unfaithfulness. Only in eternity can we rightly estimate the loss of a single soul. Fearful will be the doom of him to whom God shall say: Depart, thou wicked servant.

The voice of God is heard from heaven, declaring the day and hour of Jesus' coming, and delivering the everlasting covenant to His people. Like peals of loudest thunder His words roll through the earth. The Israel of God stand listening, with their eyes fixed upward. Their countenances are lighted up with His glory, and shine as did the face of Moses when he came down from Sinai. The wicked cannot look upon them. And when the blessing is pronounced on those who have honored God by keeping His Sabbath holy, there is a mighty shout of victory.

Soon there appears in the east a small black cloud, about half the size of a man's hand. It is the cloud which surrounds the Saviour and which seems in the distance to be shrouded in darkness. The people of God know this to be the sign of the Son of man. In solemn silence they gaze upon it as it draws nearer the earth, becoming lighter and more glorious, until it is a great white cloud, its base a glory like consuming fire, and above it the rainbow of the covenant. Jesus rides forth as a mighty conqueror. Not now a "Man of Sorrows," to drink the bitter cup of shame and woe, He comes, victor in heaven and earth, to judge the living and the dead. "Faithful and True," "in righteousness He doth judge and make war." And "the armies which were in heaven" (Revelation 19:11, 14) follow Him. With anthems of celestial melody the holy angels, a vast, unnumbered throng, attend Him on His way. The firmament seems filled with radiant forms—"ten thousand times ten thousand, and thousands of thousands." No human pen can portray the scene; no mortal mind is adequate to conceive its splendor. "His glory covered the heavens, and the earth was full of His praise. And His brightness was as the light." Habakkuk 3:3,4. As the living cloud comes still nearer, every eye beholds the Prince of life. No crown of thorns now mars that sacred head; but a diadem of glory rests on His holy brow. His countenance outshines the dazzling brightness of the noonday sun. "And He hath on His vesture and on His thigh a name written, *King of kings, and Lord of lords.*" Revelation 19:16.

Before His presence "all faces are turned into paleness;" upon the rejecters of God's mercy falls the terror of eternal despair. "The heart melteth, and the knees smite together, ... and the faces of them all gather blackness." Jeremiah 30:6; Nahum 2:10. The righteous cry with trembling: "Who shall be able to stand?" The angels' song is hushed, and there is a period of awful silence. Then the voice of Jesus is heard, saying: "My grace is sufficient for you." The faces of the righteous are lighted up, and joy fills every heart. And the angels strike a note higher and sing again as they draw still nearer to the earth.

The King of kings descends upon the cloud, wrapped in flaming fire. The heavens are rolled together as a scroll, the earth trembles before Him, and every mountain and island is moved out of its place. "Our God shall come, and shall not keep silence: a fire shall devour before Him, and it shall be very tempestuous round about Him. He shall call to the heavens from above, and to the earth, that He may judge His people." Psalm 50:3,4.

"And the kings of the earth, and the great men, and the rich men, and the chief captains, and the mighty men, and every bondman, and every freeman, hid themselves in the dens and in the rocks of the mountains; and said to the mountains and rocks, Fall on us, and hide us from the face of Him that sitteth on the throne, and from the wrath of the Lamb: for the great day of His wrath is come; and who shall be able to stand?" Revelation 6:15-17.

The derisive jests have ceased. Lying lips are hushed into silence. The clash of arms, the tumult of battle, "with confused noise, and garments rolled in blood" (Isaiah 9:5), is stilled. Nought now is heard but the voice of prayer and the sound of weeping and lamentation. The cry bursts forth from lips so lately scoffing: "The great day of His wrath is come; and who shall be able to stand?" The wicked pray to be buried beneath the rocks of the mountains rather than meet the face of Him whom they have despised and rejected.

That voice which penetrates the ear of the dead, they know. How often have its plaintive, tender tones called them to repentance. How often has it been heard in the touching entreaties of a friend, a brother, a Redeemer. To the rejecters of His grace no other could be so full of condemnation, so burdened with denunciation, as that voice which has so long pleaded: "Turn ye, turn ye from your evil ways; for why will ye die?" Ezekiel 33:11. Oh, that it were to them the voice of a stranger! Says Jesus: "I have called, and ye refused; I have stretched out My hand, and no man regarded; but ye have set at nought all My counsel, and would none of My reproof." Proverbs 1:24, 25. That voice awakens memories which they would fain blot out—warnings despised, invitations refused, privileges slighted.

There are those who mocked Christ in His humiliation. With thrilling power come to their minds the Sufferer's words, when, adjured by the high priest, He solemnly declared: "Hereafter shall ye see the Son of man sitting on the right hand of power, and coming in the clouds of heaven." Matthew 26:64. Now they behold Him in His glory, and they are yet to see Him sitting on the right hand of power.

Those who derided His claim to be the Son of God are speechless now. There is the haughty Herod who jeered at His royal title and bade the mocking soldiers crown Him king. There are the very men who with impious hands placed upon His form the purple robe, upon His sacred brow the thorny crown, and in His unresisting hand the mimic scepter, and bowed before Him in blasphemous mockery. The men who smote and spit upon the Prince of life now turn from His piercing gaze and seek to flee from the overpowering glory of His presence. Those who drove the nails through His hands and feet, the soldier who pierced His side, behold these marks with terror and remorse.

With awful distinctness do priests and rulers recall the events of Calvary. With shuddering horror they remember how, wagging their heads in satanic exultation, they exclaimed: "He saved others; Himself He cannot save. If He be the King of Israel, let Him now come down from the cross, and we will believe Him. He trusted in God; let Him deliver Him now, if He will have Him." Matthew 27:42, 43.

Vividly they recall the Saviour's parable of the husbandmen who refused to render to their lord the fruit of the vineyard, who abused his servants and slew his son. They remember, too, the sentence which they themselves pronounced: The lord of the vineyard "will miserably destroy those wicked men." In the sin and punishment of those unfaithful men the priests and elders see their own course and their own just doom. And now there rises a cry of mortal agony. Louder than the shout, "Crucify Him, crucify Him," which rang through the streets of Jerusalem, swells the awful, despairing wail, "He is the Son of God! He is the true Messiah!" They seek to flee from the presence of the King of kings. In the deep caverns of the earth, rent asunder by the warring of the elements, they vainly attempt to hide.

In the lives of all who reject truth there are moments when conscience awakens, when memory presents the torturing recollection of a life of hypocrisy and the soul is harassed with vain regrets. But what are these compared with the remorse of that day when "fear cometh as desolation," when "destruction cometh as a whirlwind"! Proverbs 1:27. Those who would have destroyed Christ and His faithful people now witness the glory which rests upon them. In the midst of their terror they hear the voices of the saints in joyful strains exclaiming: "Lo, this is our God; we have waited for Him, and He will save us." Isaiah 25:9.

Amid the reeling of the earth, the flash of lightning, and the roar of thunder, the voice of the Son of God calls forth the sleeping saints. He looks upon the graves of the righteous, then, raising His hands to heaven, He cries: "Awake, awake, awake, ye that sleep in the dust, and arise!" Throughout the length and breadth of the earth the dead shall hear that voice, and they that hear shall live. And the whole earth shall ring with the tread of the exceeding great army of every nation, kindred, tongue, and people. From the prison house of death they come, clothed with immortal glory, crying: "O death, where is thy sting? O grave, where is thy victory?" 1 Corinthians 15:55. And the living righteous and the risen saints unite their voices in a long, glad shout of victory.

All come forth from their graves the same in stature as when they entered the tomb. Adam, who stands among the risen throng, is of lofty height and majestic form, in stature but little below the Son of God. He presents a marked contrast to the people of later generations; in this one respect is shown the great degeneracy of the race. But all arise with the freshness and vigor of eternal youth. In the beginning, man was created in the likeness of God, not only in character, but in form and feature. Sin defaced and almost obliterated the divine image; but Christ came to restore that which had been lost. He will change our vile bodies and fashion them like unto His glorious body. The mortal, corruptible form, devoid of comeliness, once polluted with sin, becomes perfect, beautiful, and immortal. All blemishes and deformities are left in the grave. Restored to the tree of life in the long-lost Eden, the redeemed will "grow up" (Malachi 4:2) to the full stature of the race in its primeval glory. The last lingering traces of the curse of sin will be removed, and Christ's faithful ones will appear in "the beauty of the Lord our God," in mind and soul and body reflecting the perfect image of their Lord. Oh, wonderful redemption! long talked of, long hoped for, contemplated with eager anticipation, but never fully understood.

The living righteous are changed "in a moment, in the twinkling of an eye." At the voice of God they were glorified; now they are made immortal and with the risen saints are caught up to meet their Lord in the air. Angels "gather together His elect from the four winds, from one end of heaven to the other." Little children are borne by holy angels to their mothers' arms. Friends long separated by death are united, nevermore to part, and with songs of gladness ascend together to the City of God.

On each side of the cloudy chariot are wings, and beneath it are living wheels; and as the chariot rolls upward, the wheels cry, "Holy," and the wings, as they move, cry, "Holy," and the retinue of angels cry, "Holy, holy, holy, Lord God Almighty." And the redeemed shout, "Alleluia!" as the chariot moves onward toward the New Jerusalem.

Before entering the City of God, the Saviour bestows upon His followers the emblems of victory and invests them with the insignia of their royal state. The glittering ranks are drawn up in the form of a hollow square about their King, whose form rises in majesty high above saint and angel, whose countenance beams upon them full of benignant love. Throughout the unnumbered host of the redeemed every glance is fixed upon Him, every eye beholds His glory whose "visage was so marred more than any man, and His form more than the sons of men." Upon the heads of the overcomers, Jesus with His own right hand places the crown of glory. For each there is a crown, bearing his own "new name" (Revelation 2:17), and the inscription, "Holiness to the Lord." In every hand are placed the victor's palm and the shining harp. Then, as the commanding angels strike the note, every hand sweeps the harp strings with skillful touch, awaking sweet music in rich, melodious strains. Rapture unutterable thrills every heart, and each voice is raised in grateful praise: "Unto Him that loved us, and washed us from our sins in His own blood, and hath made us kings and priests unto God and His Father; to Him be glory and dominion for ever and ever." Revelation 1:5,6.

Before the ransomed throng is the Holy City. Jesus opens wide the pearly gates, and the nations that have kept the truth enter in. There they behold the Paradise of God, the home of Adam in his innocency. Then that voice, richer than any music that ever fell on mortal ear, is heard, saying: "Your conflict is ended." "Come, ye blessed of My Father, inherit the kingdom prepared for you from the foundation of the world."

Now is fulfilled the Saviour's prayer for His disciples: "I will that they also, whom Thou hast given Me, be with Me where I am." "Faultless before the presence of His glory with exceeding joy" (Jude 24), Christ presents to the Father the purchase of His blood, declaring: "Here am I, and the children whom Thou hast given Me." "Those that Thou gavest Me I have kept." Oh, the wonders of redeeming love! the rapture of that hour when the infinite Father, looking upon the ransomed, shall behold His image, sin's discord banished, its blight removed, and the human once more in harmony with the divine!

With unutterable love, Jesus welcomes His faithful ones to the joy of their Lord. The Saviour's joy is in seeing, in the kingdom of glory, the souls that have been saved by His agony and humiliation. And the redeemed will be sharers in His joy, as they behold, among the blessed, those who have been won to Christ through their prayers, their labors, and their loving sacrifice. As they gather about the great white throne, gladness unspeakable will fill their hearts, when they behold those whom they have won for Christ, and see that one has gained others, and these still others, all brought into the haven of rest, there to lay their crowns at Jesus' feet and praise Him through the endless cycles of eternity.

As the ransomed ones are welcomed to the City of God, there rings out upon the air an exultant cry of adoration. The two Adams are about to meet. The Son of God is standing with outstretched arms to receive the father of our race—the being whom He created, who sinned against his Maker, and for whose sin the marks of the crucifixion are borne upon the Saviour's form. As Adam discerns the prints of the cruel nails, he does not fall upon the bosom of his Lord, but in humiliation casts himself at His feet, crying: "Worthy, worthy is the Lamb that was slain!" Tenderly the Saviour lifts him up and bids him look once more upon the Eden home from which he has so long been exiled.

After his expulsion from Eden, Adam's life on earth was filled with sorrow. Every dying leaf, every victim of sacrifice, every blight upon the fair face of nature, every stain upon man's purity, was a fresh reminder of his sin. Terrible was the agony of remorse as he beheld iniquity abounding, and, in answer to his warnings, met the reproaches cast upon himself as the cause of sin. With patient humility he bore, for nearly a thousand years, the penalty of transgression. Faithfully did he repent of his sin and trust in the merits of the promised Saviour, and he died in the hope of a resurrection. The Son of God redeemed man's failure and fall; and now, through the work of the atonement, Adam is reinstated in his first dominion.

Transported with joy, he beholds the trees that were once his delight—the very trees whose fruit he himself had gathered in the days of his innocence and joy. He sees the vines that his own hands have trained, the very flowers that he once loved to care for. His mind grasps the reality of the scene; he comprehends that this is indeed Eden restored, more lovely now than when he was banished from it. The Saviour leads him to the tree of life and plucks the glorious fruit and bids him eat. He looks about him and beholds a multitude of his family redeemed, standing in the Paradise of God. Then he casts his glittering crown at the feet of Jesus and, falling upon His breast, embraces the Redeemer. He touches the golden harp, and the vaults of heaven echo the triumphant song: "Worthy, worthy, worthy is the Lamb that was slain, and lives again!" The family of Adam take up the strain and cast their crowns at the Saviour's feet as they bow before Him in adoration.

This reunion is witnessed by the angels who wept at the fall of Adam and rejoiced when Jesus, after His resurrection, ascended to heaven, having opened the grave for all who should believe on His name. Now they behold the work of redemption accomplished, and they unite their voices in the song of praise.

Upon the crystal sea before the throne, that sea of glass as it were mingled with fire,—so resplendent is it with the glory of God,—are gathered the company that have "gotten the victory over the beast, and over his image, and over his mark, and over the number of his name."

With the Lamb upon Mount Zion, "having the harps of God," they stand, the hundred and forty and four thousand that were redeemed from among men; and there is heard, as the sound of many waters, and as the sound of a great thunder, "the voice of harpers harping with their harps." And they sing "a new song" before the throne, a song which no man can learn save the hundred and forty and four thousand. It is the song of Moses and the Lamb—a song of deliverance. None but the hundred and forty-four thousand can learn that song; for it is the song of their experience—an experience such as no other company have ever had. "These are they which follow the Lamb whithersoever He goeth." These, having been translated from the earth, from among the living, are counted as "the first fruits unto God and to the Lamb." Revelation 15:2, 3; 14:1-5. "These are they which came out of great tribulation;" they have passed through the time of trouble such as never was since there was a nation; they have endured the anguish of the time of Jacob's trouble; they have stood without an intercessor through the final outpouring of God's judgments. But they have been delivered, for they have "washed their robes, and made them white in the blood of the Lamb." "In their mouth was found no guile: for they are without fault" before God. "Therefore are they before the throne of God, and serve Him day and night in His temple: and He that sitteth on the throne shall dwell among them." They have seen the earth wasted with famine and pestilence, the sun having power to scorch men with great heat, and they themselves have endured suffering, hunger, and thirst. But "they shall hunger no more, neither thirst any more; neither shall the sun light on them, nor any heat. For the Lamb which is in the midst of the throne shall feed them, and shall lead them unto living fountains of waters: and God shall wipe away all tears from their eyes." Revelation 7:14-17.

In all ages the Saviour's chosen have been educated and disciplined in the school of trial. They walked in narrow paths on earth; they were purified in the furnace of affliction. For Jesus' sake they endured opposition, hatred, calumny. They followed Him through conflicts sore; they endured self-denial and experienced bitter disappointments. By their own painful experience they learned the evil of sin, its power, its guilt, its woe; and they look upon it with abhorrence. A sense of the infinite sacrifice made for its cure humbles them in their own sight and fills their hearts with gratitude and praise which those who have never fallen cannot appreciate. They love much because they have been forgiven much. Having been partakers of Christ's sufferings, they are fitted to be partakers with Him of His glory.

The heirs of God have come from garrets, from hovels, from dungeons, from scaffolds, from mountains, from deserts, from the caves of the earth, from the caverns of the sea. On earth they were "destitute, afflicted, tormented." Millions went down to the grave loaded with infamy because they steadfastly refused to yield to the deceptive claims of Satan. By human tribunals they were adjudged the vilest of criminals. But now "God is judge Himself," Psalm 50:6. Now the decisions of earth are reversed. "The rebuke of His people shall He take away," Isaiah 25:8. "They shall call them, The holy people, The redeemed of the Lord." He hath appointed "to give unto them beauty for ashes, the oil of joy for mourning, the garment of praise for the spirit of heaviness." Isaiah 62:12; 61:3. They are no longer feeble, afflicted, scattered, and oppressed. Henceforth they are to be ever with the Lord. They stand before the throne clad in richer robes than the most honored of the earth have ever worn. They are crowned with diadems more glorious than were ever placed upon the brow of earthly monarchs. The days of pain and weeping are forever ended. The King of glory has wiped the tears from all faces; every cause of grief has been removed. Amid the waving of palm branches they pour forth a song of praise, clear, sweet, and harmonious; every voice takes up the strain, until the anthem swells through the vaults of heaven: "Salvation to our God which sitteth upon the throne, and unto the Lamb." And all the inhabitants of heaven respond in the ascription: "Amen: Blessing, and glory, and wisdom, and thanksgiving, and honor, and power, and might, be unto our God for ever and ever." Revelation 7:10, 12.

In this life we can only begin to understand the wonderful theme of redemption. With our finite comprehension we may consider most earnestly the shame and the glory, the life and the death, the justice and the mercy, that meet in the cross; yet with the utmost stretch of our mental powers we fail to grasp its full significance. The length and the breadth, the depth and the height, of redeeming love are but dimly comprehended. The plan of redemption will not be fully understood, even when the ransomed see as they are seen and know as they are known; but through the eternal ages new truth will continually unfold to the wondering and delighted mind. Though the griefs and pains and temptations of earth are ended and the cause removed, the people of God will ever have a distinct, intelligent knowledge of what their salvation has cost.

The cross of Christ will be the science and the song of the redeemed through all eternity. In Christ glorified they will behold Christ crucified. Never will it be forgotten that He whose power created and upheld the unnumbered worlds through the vast realms of space, the Beloved of God, the Majesty of heaven, He whom cherub and shining seraph delighted to adore—humbled Himself to uplift fallen man; that He bore the guilt and shame of sin, and the hiding of His Father's face, till the woes of a lost world broke His heart and crushed out His life on Calvary's cross. That the Maker of all worlds, the Arbiter of all destinies, should lay aside His glory and humiliate Himself from love to man will ever excite the wonder and adoration of the universe. As the nations of the saved look upon their Redeemer and behold the eternal glory of the Father shining in His countenance; as they behold His throne, which is from everlasting to everlasting, and know that His kingdom is to have no end, they break forth in rapturous song: "Worthy, worthy is the Lamb that was slain, and hath redeemed us to God by His own most precious blood!"

The mystery of the cross explains all other mysteries. In the light that streams from Calvary the attributes of God which had filled us with fear and awe appear beautiful and attractive. Mercy, tenderness, and parental love are seen to blend with holiness, justice, and power. While we behold the majesty of His throne, high and lifted up, we see His character in its gracious manifestations, and comprehend, as never before, the significance of that endearing title, "Our Father."

It will be seen that He who is infinite in wisdom could devise no plan for our salvation except the sacrifice of His Son. The compensation for this sacrifice is the joy of peopling the earth with ransomed beings, holy, happy, and immortal. The result of the Saviour's conflict with the powers of darkness is joy to the redeemed, redounding to the glory of God throughout eternity. And such is the value of the soul that the Father is satisfied with the price paid; and Christ Himself, beholding the fruits of His great sacrifice, is satisfied.

Nine

—Desolation of the Earth—

"Her sins have reached unto heaven, and God hath remembered her iniquities. ... In the cup which she hath filled fill to her double. How much she hath glorified herself, and lived deliciously, so much torment and sorrow give her: for she saith in her heart, I sit a queen, and am no widow, and shall see no sorrow. Therefore shall her plagues come in one day, death, and mourning, and famine; and she shall be utterly burned with fire: for strong is the Lord God who judgeth her. And the kings of the earth, who have committed fornication and lived deliciously with her, shall bewail her, and lament for her, ... saying, Alas, alas that great city Babylon, that mighty city! for in one hour is thy judgment come." Revelation 18:5-10.

"The merchants of the earth," that have "waxed rich through the abundance of her delicacies," "shall stand afar off for the fear of her torment, weeping and wailing, and saying, Alas, alas that great city, that was clothed in fine linen, and purple, and scarlet, and decked with gold, and precious stones, and pearls! For in one hour so great riches is come to nought." Revelation 18:11, 3, 15-17.

Such are the judgments that fall upon Babylon in the day of the visitation of God's wrath. She has filled up the measure of her iniquity; her time has come; she is ripe for destruction.

When the voice of God turns the captivity of His people, there is a terrible awakening of those who have lost all in the great conflict of life. While probation continued they were blinded by Satan's deceptions, and they justified their course of sin. The rich prided themselves upon their superiority to those who were less favored; but they had obtained their riches by violation of the law of God. They had neglected to feed the hungry, to clothe the naked, to deal justly, and to love mercy. They had sought to exalt themselves and to obtain the homage of their fellow creatures. Now they are stripped of all that made them great and are left destitute and defenseless. They look with terror upon the destruction of the idols which they preferred before their Maker. They have sold their souls for earthly riches and enjoyments, and have not sought to become rich toward God. The result is, their lives are a failure; their pleasures are now turned to gall, their treasures to corruption. The gain of a lifetime is swept away in a moment. The rich bemoan the destruction of their grand houses, the scattering of their gold and silver. But their lamentations are silenced by the fear that they themselves are to perish with their idols.

The wicked are filled with regret, not because of their sinful neglect of God and their fellow men, but because God has conquered. They lament that the result is what it is; but they do not repent of their wickedness. They would leave no means untried to conquer if they could.

The world see the very class whom they have mocked and derided, and desired to exterminate, pass unharmed through pestilence, tempest, and earthquake. He who is to the transgressors of His law a devouring fire, is to His people a safe pavilion.

The minister who has sacrificed truth to gain the favor of men now discerns the character and influence of his teachings. It is apparent that the omniscient eye was following him as he stood in the desk, as he walked the streets, as he mingled with men in the various scenes of life. Every emotion of the soul, every line written, every word uttered, every act that led men to rest in a refuge of falsehood, has been scattering seed; and now, in the wretched, lost souls around him, he beholds the harvest.

Saith the Lord: "They have healed the hurt of the daughter of My people slightly, saying, Peace, peace; when there is no peace." "With lies ye have made the heart of the righteous sad, whom I have not made sad; and strengthened the hands of the wicked, that he should not return from his wicked way, by promising him life." Jeremiah 8:11; Ezekiel 13:22.

"Woe be unto the pastors that destroy and scatter the sheep of My pasture! Behold, I will visit upon you the evil of your doings." "Howl, ye shepherds, and cry; and wallow yourselves in the ashes, ye principal of the flock: for your days for slaughter and of your dispersions are accomplished; and the shepherds shall have no way to flee, nor the principal of the flock to escape." Jeremiah 23:1, 2; 25:34, 35, margin.

Ministers and people see that they have not sustained the right relation to God. They see that they have rebelled against the Author of all just and righteous law. The setting aside of the divine precepts gave rise to thousands of springs of evil, discord, hatred, iniquity, until the earth became one vast field of strife, one sink of corruption. This is the view that now appears to those who rejected truth and chose to cherish error. No language can express the longing which the disobedient and disloyal feel for that which they have lost forever—eternal life. Men whom the world has worshiped for their talents and eloquence now see these things in their true light. They realize what they have forfeited by transgression, and they fall at the feet of those whose fidelity they have despised and derided, and confess that God has loved them.

The people see that they have been deluded. They accuse one another of having led them to destruction; but all unite in heaping their bitterest condemnation upon the ministers. Unfaithful pastors have prophesied smooth things; they have led their hearers to make void the law of God and to persecute those who would keep it holy. Now, in their despair, these teachers confess before the world their work of deception. The multitudes are filled with fury. "We are lost!" they cry, "and you are the cause of our ruin;" and they turn upon the false shepherds. The very ones that once admired them most will pronounce the most dreadful curses upon them. The very hands that once crowned them with laurels will be raised for their destruction. The swords which were to slay God's people are now employed to destroy their enemies. Everywhere there is strife and bloodshed.

"A noise shall come even to the ends of the earth; for the Lord hath a controversy with the nations, He will plead with all flesh; He will give them that are wicked to the sword." Jeremiah 25:31. For six thousand years the great controversy has been in progress; the Son of God and His heavenly messengers have been in conflict with the power of the evil one, to warn, enlighten, and save the children of men. Now all have made their decisions; the wicked have fully united with Satan in his warfare against God. The time has come for God to vindicate the authority of His downtrodden law. Now the controversy is not alone with Satan, but with men. "The Lord hath a controversy with the nations;" "He will give them that are wicked to the sword."

The mark of deliverance has been set upon those "that sigh and that cry for all the abominations that be done." Now the angel of death goes forth, represented in Ezekiel's vision by the men with the slaughtering weapons, to whom the command is given: "Slay utterly old and young, both maids, and little children, and women: but come not near any man upon whom is the mark; and begin at My sanctuary." Says the prophet: "They began at the ancient men which were before the house." Ezekiel 9:1-6. The work of destruction begins among those who have professed to be the spiritual guardians of the people. The false watchmen are the first to fall. There are none to pity or to spare. Men, women, maidens, and little children perish together.

"The Lord cometh out of His place to punish the inhabitants of the earth for their iniquity: the earth also shall disclose her blood, and shall no more cover her slain." Isaiah 26:21. "And this shall be the plague wherewith the Lord will smite all the people that have fought against Jerusalem; Their flesh shall consume away while they stand upon their feet, and their eyes shall consume away in their holes, and their tongue shall consume away in their mouth. And it shall come to pass in that day, that a great tumult from the Lord shall be among them; and they shall lay hold everyone on the hand of his neighbor, and his hand shall rise up against the hand of his neighbor." Zechariah 14:12, 13. In the mad strife of their own fierce passions, and by the awful outpouring of God's unmingled wrath, fall the wicked inhabitants of the earth—priests, rulers, and people, rich and poor, high and low. "And the slain of the Lord shall be at that day from one end of the earth even unto the other end of the earth: they shall not be lamented, neither gathered, nor buried." Jeremiah 25:33.

At the coming of Christ the wicked are blotted from the face of the whole earth—consumed with the spirit of His mouth and destroyed by the brightness of His glory. Christ takes His people to the City of God, and the earth is emptied of its inhabitants. "Behold, the Lord maketh the earth empty, and maketh it waste, and turneth it upside down, and scattereth abroad the inhabitants thereof." "The land shall be utterly emptied, and utterly spoiled: for the Lord hath spoken this word." "Because they have transgressed the laws, changed the ordinance, broken the everlasting covenant. Therefore hath the curse devoured the earth, and they that dwell therein are desolate: therefore the inhabitants of the earth are burned." Isaiah 24:1, 3, 5, 6.

The whole earth appears like a desolate wilderness. The ruins of cities and villages destroyed by the earthquake, uprooted trees, ragged rocks thrown out by the sea or torn out of the earth itself, are scattered over its surface, while vast caverns mark the spot where the mountains have been rent from their foundations.

Now the event takes place foreshadowed in the last solemn service of the Day of Atonement. When the ministration in the holy of holies had been completed, and the sins of Israel had been removed from the sanctuary by virtue of the blood of the sin offering, then the scapegoat was presented alive before the Lord; and in the presence of the congregation the high priest confessed over him "all the iniquities of the children of Israel, and all their transgressions in all their sins, putting them upon the head of the goat." Leviticus 16:21. In like manner, when the work of atonement in the heavenly sanctuary has been completed, then in the presence of God and heavenly angels and the hosts of the redeemed the sins of God's people will be placed upon Satan; he will be declared guilty of all the evil which he has caused them to commit. And as the scapegoat was sent away into a land not inhabited, so Satan will be banished to the desolate earth, an uninhabited and dreary wilderness.

The revelator foretells the banishment of Satan and the condition of chaos and desolation to which the earth is to be reduced, and he declares that this condition will exist for a thousand years. After presenting the scenes of the Lord's second coming and the destruction of the wicked, the prophecy continues: "I saw an angel come down from heaven, having the key of the bottomless pit and a great chain in his hand. And he laid hold on the dragon, that old serpent, which is the devil, and Satan, and bound him a thousand years, and cast him into the bottomless pit, and shut him up, and set a seal upon him, that he should deceive the nations no more, till the thousand years should be fulfilled: and after that he must be loosed a little season." Revelation 20:1-3.

That the expression "bottomless pit" represents the earth in a state of confusion and darkness is evident from other scriptures. Concerning the condition of the earth "in the beginning," the Bible record says that it "was without form, and void; and darkness was upon the face of the deep." Genesis 1:2. Prophecy teaches that it will be brought back, partially at least, to this condition. Looking forward to the great day of God, the prophet Jeremiah declares: "I beheld the earth, and, lo, it was without form, and void; and the heavens, and they had no light. I beheld the mountains, and, lo, they trembled, and all the hills moved lightly.

I beheld, and, lo, there was no man, and all the birds of the heavens were fled. I beheld, and, lo, the fruitful place was a wilderness, and all the cities thereof were broken down." Jeremiah 4:23-26.

Here is to be the home of Satan with his evil angels for a thousand years. Limited to the earth, he will not have access to other worlds to tempt and annoy those who have never fallen. It is in this sense that he is bound: there are none remaining, upon whom he can exercise his power. He is wholly cut off from the work of deception and ruin which for so many centuries has been his sole delight.

The prophet Isaiah, looking forward to the time of Satan's overthrow, exclaims: "How art thou fallen from heaven, O Lucifer, son of the morning! how art thou cut down to the ground, which didst weaken the nations! . . . Thou hast said in thine heart, I will ascend into heaven, I will exalt my throne above the stars of God: . . . I will be like the Most High. Yet thou shalt be brought down to hell, to the sides of the pit. They that see thee shall narrowly look upon thee, and consider thee, saying, Is this the man that made the earth to tremble, that did shake kingdoms; that made the world as a wilderness, and destroyed the cities thereof; that opened not the house of his prisoners?" Isaiah 14:12-17.

For six thousand years, Satan's work of rebellion has "made the earth to tremble." He has "made the world as a wilderness, and destroyed the cities thereof." And he "opened not the house of his prisoners." For six thousand years his prison house has received God's people, and he would have held them captive forever; but Christ had broken his bonds and set the prisoners free.

Even the wicked are now placed beyond the power of Satan, and alone with his evil angels he remains to realize the effect of the curse which sin has brought. "The kings of the nations, even all of them, lie in glory, everyone in his own house [the grave]. But thou art cast out of thy grave like an abominable branch. . . . Thou shalt not be joined with them in burial, because thou hast destroyed thy land, and slain thy people." Isaiah 14:18-20.

For a thousand years, Satan will wander to and fro in the desolate earth to behold the results of his rebellion against the law of God. During this time his sufferings are intense. Since his fall his life of unceasing activity has banished reflection; but he is now deprived of his power and left to contemplate the part which he has acted since first he rebelled against the government of heaven, and to look forward with trembling and terror to the dreadful future when he must suffer for all the evil that he has done and be punished for the sins that he has caused to be committed.

To God's people the captivity of Satan will bring gladness and rejoicing. Says the prophet: "It shall come to pass in the day that Jehovah shall give thee rest from thy sorrow, and from thy trouble, and from the hard service wherein thou wast made to serve, that thou shalt take up this parable against the king of Babylon [here representing Satan], and say, How hath the oppressor ceased! ... Jehovah hath broken the staff of the wicked, the scepter of the rulers; that smote the peoples in wrath with a continual stroke, that ruled the nations in anger, with a persecution that none restrained." Verses 3-6, R.V.

During the thousand years between the first and the second resurrection the judgment of the wicked takes place. The apostle Paul points to this judgment as an event that follows the second advent. "Judge nothing before the time, until the Lord come, who both will bring to light the hidden things of darkness, and will make manifest the counsels of the hearts." 1 Corinthians 4:5. Daniel declares that when the Ancient of Days came, "judgment was given to the saints of the Most High." Daniel 7:22. At this time the righteous reign as kings and priests unto God. John in the Revelation says: "I saw thrones, and they sat upon them, and judgment was given unto them." "They shall be priests of God and of Christ, and shall reign with Him a thousand years." Revelation 20:4, 6. It is at this time that, as foretold by Paul, "the saints shall judge the world." 1 Corinthians 6:2. In union with Christ they judge the wicked, comparing their acts with the statute book, the Bible, and deciding every case according to the deeds done in the body. Then the portion which the wicked must suffer is meted out, according to their works; and it is recorded against their names in the book of death.

Satan also and evil angels are judged by Christ and His people. Says Paul: "Know ye not that we shall judge angels?" Verse 3. And Jude declares that "the angels which kept not their first estate, but left their own habitation, He hath reserved in everlasting chains under darkness unto the judgment of the great day." Jude 6.

At the close of the thousand years the second resurrection will take place. Then the wicked will be raised from the dead and appear before God for the execution of "the judgment written." Thus the revelator, after describing the resurrection of the righteous, says: "The rest of the dead lived not again until the thousand years were finished." Revelation 20:5. And Isaiah declares, concerning the wicked: "They shall be gathered together, as prisoners are gathered in the pit, and shall be shut up in the prison, and *after many days shall they be visited.*" Isaiah 24:22.

Ten

—The Controversy Ended—

A t the close of the thousand years, Christ again returns to the earth. He is accompanied by the host of the redeemed and attended by a retinue of angels. As He descends in terrific majesty He bids the wicked dead arise to receive their doom. They come forth, a mighty host, numberless as the sands of the sea. What a contrast to those who were raised at the first resurrection! The righteous were clothed with immortal youth and beauty. The wicked bear the traces of disease and death.

Every eye in that vast multitude is turned to behold the glory of the Son of God. With one voice the wicked hosts exclaim: "Blessed is He that cometh in the name of the Lord!" It is not love to Jesus that inspires this utterance. The force of truth urges the words from unwilling lips. As the wicked went into their graves, so they come forth with the same enmity to Christ and the same spirit of rebellion. They are to have no new probation in which to remedy the defects of their past lives. Nothing would be gained by this. A lifetime of transgression has not softened their hearts. A second probation, were it given them, would be occupied as was the first in evading the requirements of God and exciting rebellion against Him.

Christ descends upon the Mount of Olives, whence, after His resurrection, He ascended, and where angels repeated the promise of His return. Says the prophet: "The Lord my God shall come, and all the saints with Thee." "And His feet shall stand in that day upon the Mount of Olives, which is before Jerusalem on the east, and the Mount of Olives shall cleave in the midst thereof, ... and there shall be a very great valley." "And the Lord shall be king over all the earth: in that day shall there be one Lord, and His name one." Zechariah 14:5, 4, 9. As the New Jerusalem, in its dazzling splendor, comes down out of heaven, it rests upon the place purified and made ready to receive it, and Christ, with His people and the angels, enters the Holy City.

Now Satan prepares for a last mighty struggle for the supremacy. While deprived of his power and cut off from his work of deception, the prince of evil was miserable and dejected; but as the wicked dead are raised and he sees the vast multitudes upon his side, his hopes revive, and he determines not to yield the great controversy. He will marshal all the armies of the lost under his banner and through them endeavor to execute his plans. The wicked are Satan's captives. In rejecting Christ they have accepted the rule of the rebel leader. They are ready to receive his suggestions and to do his bidding. Yet, true to his early cunning, he does not acknowledge himself to be Satan. He claims to be the prince who is the rightful owner of the world and whose inheritance has been unlawfully wrested from him. He represents himself to his deluded subjects as a redeemer, assuring them that his power has brought them forth from their graves and that he is about to rescue them from the most cruel tyranny. The presence of Christ having been removed, Satan works wonders to support his claims. He makes the weak strong and inspires all with his own spirit and energy. He proposes to lead them against the camp of the saints and to take possession of the City of God. With fiendish exultation he points to the unnumbered millions who have been raised from the dead and declares that as their leader he is well able to overthrow the city and regain his throne and his kingdom.

In that vast throng are multitudes of the long-lived race that existed before the Flood; men of lofty stature and giant intellect, who, yielding to the control of fallen angels, devoted all their skill and knowledge to the exaltation of themselves; men whose wonderful works of art led the world to idolize their genius, but whose cruelty and evil inventions, defiling the earth and defacing the image of God, caused Him to blot them from the face of His creation. There are kings and generals who conquered nations, valiant men who never lost a battle, proud, ambitious warriors whose approach made kingdoms tremble. In death these experienced no change. As they come up from the grave, they resume the current of their thoughts just where it ceased. They are actuated by the same desire to conquer that ruled them when they fell.

Satan consults with his angels, and then with these kings and conquerors and mighty men. They look upon the strength and numbers on their side, and declare that the army within the city is small in comparison with theirs, and that it can be overcome. They lay their plans to take possession of the riches and glory of the New Jerusalem. All immediately begin to prepare for battle. Skillful artisans construct implements of war. Military leaders, famed for their success, marshal the throngs of warlike men into companies and divisions.

At last the order to advance is given, and the countless host moves on—an army such as was never summoned by earthly conquerors, such as the combined forces of all ages since war began on earth could never equal. Satan, the mightiest of warriors, leads the van, and his angels unite their forces for this final struggle. Kings and warriors are in his train, and the multitudes follow in vast companies, each under its appointed leader. With military precision the serried ranks advance over the earth's broken and uneven surface to the City of God. By command of Jesus, the gates of the New Jerusalem are closed, and the armies of Satan surround the city and make ready for the onset.

Now Christ again appears to the view of His enemies. Far above the city, upon a foundation of burnished gold, is a throne, high and lifted up. Upon this throne sits the Son of God, and around Him are the subjects of His kingdom. The power and majesty of Christ no language can describe, no pen portray. The glory of the Eternal Father is enshrouding His Son. The brightness of His presence fills the City of God, and flows out beyond the gates, flooding the whole earth with its radiance.

Nearest the throne are those who were once zealous in the cause of Satan, but who, plucked as brands from the burning, have followed their Saviour with deep, intense devotion. Next are those who perfected Christian characters in the midst of falsehood and infidelity, those who honored the law of God when the Christian world declared it void, and the millions, of all ages, who were martyred for their faith. And beyond is the "great multitude, which no man could number, of all nations, and kindreds, and people, and tongues, ... before the throne, and before the Lamb, clothed with white robes, and palms in their hands." Revelation 7:9. Their warfare is ended, their victory won. They have run the race, and reached the prize. The palm branch in their hands is a symbol of their triumph, the white robe an emblem of the spotless righteousness of Christ which now is theirs.

The redeemed raise a song of praise that echoes and re-echoes through the vaults of heaven: "Salvation to our God which sitteth upon the throne, and unto the Lamb." Verse 10. And angel and seraph unite their voices in adoration. As the redeemed have beheld the power and malignity of Satan, they have seen, as never before, that no power but that of Christ could have made them conquerors. In all that shining throng there are none to ascribe salvation to themselves, as if they had prevailed by their own power and goodness. Nothing is said of what they have done or suffered; but the burden of every song, the keynote of every anthem, is: Salvation to our God and unto the Lamb.

In the presence of the assembled inhabitants of earth and heaven the final coronation of the Son of God takes place. And now, invested with supreme majesty and power, the King of kings pronounces sentence upon the rebels against His government and executes justice upon those who have transgressed His law and oppressed His people. Says the prophet of God: "I saw a great white throne, and Him that sat on it, from whose face the earth and the heaven fled away; and there was found no place for them. And I saw the dead, small and great, stand before God; and the books were opened: and another book was opened, which is the book of life: and the dead were judged out of those things which were written in the books, according to their works." Revelation 20:11, 12.

As soon as the books of record are opened, and the eye of Jesus looks upon the wicked, they are conscious of every sin which they have ever committed. They see just where their feet diverged from the path of purity and holiness, just how far pride and rebellion have carried them in the violation of the law of God. The seductive temptations which they encouraged by indulgence in sin, the blessings perverted, the messengers of God despised, the warnings rejected, the waves of mercy beaten back by the stubborn, unrepentant heart—all appear as if written in letters of fire.

Above the throne is revealed the cross; and like a panoramic view appear the scenes of Adam's temptation and fall, and the successive steps in the great plan of redemption. The Saviour's lowly birth; His early life of simplicity and obedience; His baptism in Jordan; the fast and temptation in the wilderness; His public ministry, unfolding to men heaven's most precious blessings; the days crowded with deeds of love and mercy, the nights of prayer and watching in the solitude of the mountains; the plottings of envy, hate, and malice which repaid His benefits; the awful, mysterious agony in Gethsemane beneath the crushing weight of the sins of the whole world; His betrayal into the hands of the murderous mob; the fearful events of that night of horror—the unresisting prisoner, forsaken by His best-loved disciples, rudely hurried through the streets of Jerusalem; the Son of God exultingly displayed before Annas, arraigned in the high priest's palace, in the judgment hall of Pilate, before the cowardly and cruel Herod, mocked, insulted, tortured, and condemned to die—all are vividly portrayed.

And now before the swaying multitude are revealed the final scenes—the patient Sufferer treading the path to Calvary; the Prince of heaven hanging upon the cross; the haughty priests and the jeering rabble deriding His expiring agony; the supernatural darkness; the heaving earth, the rent rocks, the open graves, marking the moment when the world's Redeemer yielded up His life.

The awful spectacle appears just as it was. Satan, his angels, and his subjects have no power to turn from the picture of their own work. Each actor recalls the part which he performed. Herod, who slew the innocent children of Bethlehem that he might destroy the King of Israel; the base Herodias, upon whose guilty soul rests the blood of John the Baptist; the weak, timeserving Pilate; the mocking soldiers; the priests and rulers and the maddened throng who cried, "His blood be on us, and on our children!"—all behold the enormity of their guilt. They vainly seek to hide from the divine majesty of His countenance, outshining the glory of the sun, while the redeemed cast their crowns at the Saviour's feet, exclaiming: "He died for me!"

Amid the ransomed throng are the apostles of Christ, the heroic Paul, the ardent Peter, the loved and loving John, and their truehearted brethren, and with them the vast host of martyrs; while outside the walls, with every vile and abominable thing, are those by whom they were persecuted, imprisoned, and slain. There is Nero, that monster of cruelty and vice, beholding the joy and exaltation of those whom he once tortured, and in whose extremest anguish he found satanic delight. His mother is there to witness the result of her own work; to see how the evil stamp of character transmitted to her son, the passions encouraged and developed by her influence and example, have borne fruit in crimes that caused the world to shudder.

There are papist priests and prelates, who claimed to be Christ's ambassadors, yet employed the rack, the dungeon, and the stake to control the consciences of His people. There are the proud pontiffs who exalted themselves above God and presumed to change the law of the Most High. Those pretended fathers of the church have an account to render to God from which they would fain be excused. Too late they are made to see that the Omniscient One is jealous of His law and that He will in no wise clear the guilty. They learn now that Christ identifies His interest with that of His suffering people; and they feel the force of His own words: "Inasmuch as ye have done it unto one of the least of these My brethren, ye have done it unto Me." Matthew 25:40.

The whole wicked world stand arraigned at the bar of God on the charge of high treason against the government of heaven. They have none to plead their cause; they are without excuse; and the sentence of eternal death is pronounced against them.

It is now evident to all that the wages of sin is not noble independence and eternal life, but slavery, ruin, and death. The wicked see what they have forfeited by their life of rebellion. The far more exceeding and eternal weight of glory was despised when offered them; but how desirable it now appears. "All this," cries the lost soul, "I might have had; but I chose to put these things far from me. Oh, strange infatuation! I have exchanged peace, happiness, and honor for wretchedness, infamy, and despair." All see that their exclusion from heaven is just. By their lives they have declared: "We will not have this Man [Jesus] to reign over us."

As if entranced, the wicked have looked upon the coronation of the Son of God. They see in His hands the tables of the divine law, the statutes which they have despised and transgressed. They witness the outburst of wonder, rapture, and adoration from the saved; and as the wave of melody sweeps over the multitudes without the city, all with one voice exclaim, "Great and marvelous are Thy works, Lord God Almighty; just and true are Thy ways, Thou King of saints" (Revelation 15:3); and, falling prostrate, they worship the Prince of life.

Satan seems paralyzed as he beholds the glory and majesty of Christ. He who was once a covering cherub remembers whence he has fallen. A shining seraph, "son of the morning;" how changed, how degraded! From the council where once he was honored, he is forever excluded. He sees another now standing near to the Father, veiling His glory. He has seen the crown placed upon the head of Christ by an angel of lofty stature and majestic presence, and he knows that the exalted position of this angel might have been his.

Memory recalls the home of his innocence and purity, the peace and content that were his until he indulged in murmuring against God, and envy of Christ. His accusations, his rebellion, his deceptions to gain the sympathy and support of the angels, his stubborn persistence in making no effort for self-recovery when God would have granted him forgiveness—all come vividly before him. He reviews his work among men and its results—the enmity of man toward his fellow man, the terrible destruction of life, the rise and fall of kingdoms, the overturning of thrones, the long succession of tumults, conflicts, and revolutions. He recalls his constant efforts to oppose the work of Christ and to sink man lower and lower. He sees that his hellish plots have been powerless to destroy those who have put their trust in Jesus. As Satan looks upon his kingdom, the fruit of his toil, he sees only failure and ruin. He has led the multitudes to believe that the City of God would be an easy prey; but he knows that this is false. Again and again, in the progress of the great controversy, he has been defeated and compelled to yield. He knows too well the power and majesty of the Eternal.

The aim of the great rebel has ever been to justify himself and to prove the divine government responsible for the rebellion. To this end he has bent all the power of his giant intellect. He has worked deliberately and systematically, and with marvelous success, leading vast multitudes to accept his version of the great controversy which has been so long in progress. For thousands of years this chief of conspiracy has palmed off falsehood for truth. But the time has now come when the rebellion is to be finally defeated and the history and character of Satan disclosed. In his last great effort to dethrone Christ, destroy His people, and take possession of the City of God, the archdeceiver has been fully unmasked. Those who have united with him see the total failure of his cause. Christ's followers and the loyal angels behold the full extent of his machinations against the government of God. He is the object of universal abhorrence. Satan sees that his voluntary rebellion has unfitted him for heaven. He has trained his powers to war against God; the purity, peace, and harmony of heaven would be to him supreme torture. His accusations against the mercy and justice of God are now silenced. The reproach which he has endeavored to cast upon Jehovah rests wholly upon himself. And now Satan bows down and confesses the justice of his sentence.

"Who shall not fear Thee, O Lord, and glorify Thy name? for Thou only art holy: for all nations shall come and worship before Thee; for Thy judgments are made manifest." Verse 4. Every question of truth and error in the long-standing controversy has now been made plain. The results of rebellion, the fruits of setting aside the divine statutes, have been laid open to the view of all created intelligences. The working out of Satan's rule in contrast with the government of God has been presented to the whole universe. Satan's own works have condemned him. God's wisdom, His justice, and His goodness stand fully vindicated. It is seen that all His dealings in the great controversy have been conducted with respect to the eternal good of His people and the good of all the worlds that He has created. "All Thy works shall praise Thee, O Lord; and Thy saints shall bless Thee." Psalm 145:10. The history of sin will stand to all eternity as a witness that with the existence of God's law is bound up the happiness of all the beings He has created. With all the facts of the great controversy in view, the whole universe, both loyal and rebellious, with one accord declare: "Just and true are Thy ways, Thou King of saints."

Before the universe has been clearly presented the great sacrifice made by the Father and the Son in man's behalf. The hour has come when Christ occupies His rightful position and is glorified above principalities and powers and every name that is named. It was for the joy that was set before Him—that He might bring many sons unto glory—that He endured the cross and despised the shame. And inconceivably great as was the sorrow and the shame, yet greater is the joy and the glory. He looks upon the redeemed, renewed in His own image, every heart bearing the perfect impress of the divine, every face reflecting the likeness of their King. He beholds in them the result of the travail of His soul, and He is satisfied. Then, in a voice that reaches the assembled multitudes of the righteous and the wicked, He declares: "Behold the purchase of My blood! For these I suffered, for these I died, that they might dwell in My presence throughout eternal ages." And the song of praise ascends from the white-robed ones about the throne: "Worthy is the Lamb that was slain to receive power, and riches, and wisdom, and strength, and honor, and glory, and blessing." Revelation 5:12.

Notwithstanding that Satan has been constrained to acknowledge God's justice and to bow to the supremacy of Christ, his character remains unchanged. The spirit of rebellion, like a mighty torrent, again bursts forth. Filled with frenzy, he determines not to yield the great controversy. The time has come for a last desperate struggle against the King of heaven. He rushes into the midst of his subjects and endeavors to inspire them with his own fury and arouse them to instant battle. But of all the countless millions whom he has allured into rebellion, there are none now to acknowledge his supremacy. His power is at an end. The wicked are filled with the same hatred of God that inspires Satan; but they see that their case is hopeless, that they cannot prevail against Jehovah. Their rage is kindled against Satan and those who have been his agents in deception, and with the fury of demons they turn upon them.

Saith the Lord: "Because thou hast set thine heart as the heart of God; behold, therefore I will bring strangers upon thee, the terrible of the nations: and they shall draw their swords against the beauty of thy wisdom, and they shall defile thy brightness. They shall bring thee down to the pit." "I will destroy thee, O covering cherub, from the midst of the stones of fire. ... I will cast thee to the ground, I will lay thee before kings, that they may behold thee. ... I will bring thee to ashes upon the earth in the sight of all them that behold thee. ... Thou shalt be a terror, and never shalt thou be any more." Ezekiel 28:6-8, 16-19.

"Every battle of the warrior is with confused noise, and garments rolled in blood; but this shall be with burning and fuel of fire." "The indignation of the Lord is upon all nations, and His fury upon all their armies: He hath utterly destroyed them, He hath delivered them to the slaughter." "Upon the wicked He shall rain quick burning coals, fire and brimstone and an horrible tempest: this shall be the portion of their cup." Isaiah 9:5; 34:2; Psalm 11:6, margin. Fire comes down from God out of heaven. The earth is broken up. The weapons concealed in its depths are drawn forth. Devouring flames burst from every yawning chasm. The very rocks are on fire. The day has come that shall burn as an oven. The elements melt with fervent heat, the earth also, and the works that are therein are burned up. Malachi 4:1; 2 Peter 3:10. The earth's surface seems one molten mass—a vast, seething lake of fire. It is the time of the judgment and perdition of ungodly men—"the day of the Lord's vengeance, and the year of recompenses for the controversy of Zion." Isaiah 34:8.

The wicked receive their recompense in the earth. Proverbs 11:31. They "shall be stubble: and the day that cometh shall burn them up, saith the Lord of hosts." Malachi 4:1. Some are destroyed as in a moment, while others suffer many days. All are punished "according to their deeds." The sins of the righteous having been transferred to Satan, he is made to suffer not only for his own rebellion, but for all the sins which he has caused God's people to commit. His punishment is to be far greater than that of those whom he has deceived. After all have perished who fell by his deceptions, he is still to live and suffer on. In the cleansing flames the wicked are at last destroyed, root and branch—Satan the root, his followers the branches. The full penalty of the law has been visited; the demands of justice have been met; and heaven and earth, beholding, declare the righteousness of Jehovah.

Satan's work of ruin is forever ended. For six thousand years he has wrought his will, filling the earth with woe and causing grief throughout the universe. The whole creation has groaned and travailed together in pain. Now God's creatures are forever delivered from his presence and temptations. "The whole earth is at rest, and is quiet: they [the righteous] break forth into singing." Isaiah 14:7. And a shout of praise and triumph ascends from the whole loyal universe. "The voice of a great multitude," "as the voice of many waters, and as the voice of mighty thunderings," is heard, saying: "Alleluia: for the Lord God omnipotent reigneth." Revelation 19:6.

While the earth was wrapped in the fire of destruction, the righteous abode safely in the Holy City. Upon those that had part in the first resurrection, the second death has no power. While God is to the wicked a consuming fire, He is to His people both a sun and a shield. Revelation 20:6; Psalm 84:11.

"I saw a new heaven and a new earth: for the first heaven and the first earth were passed away." Revelation 21:1. The fire that consumes the wicked purifies the earth. Every trace of the curse is swept away. No eternally burning hell will keep before the ransomed the fearful consequences of sin.

One reminder alone remains: Our Redeemer will ever bear the marks of His crucifixion. Upon His wounded head, upon His side, His hands and feet, are the only traces of the cruel work that sin has wrought. Says the prophet, beholding Christ in His glory: "He had bright beams coming out of His side: and there was the hiding of His power." Habakkuk 3:4, margin. That pierced side whence flowed the crimson stream that reconciled man to God—there is the Saviour's glory, there "the hiding of His power." "Mighty to save," through the sacrifice of redemption, He was therefore strong to execute justice upon them that despised God's mercy. And the tokens of His humiliation are His highest honor; through the eternal ages the wounds of Calvary will show forth His praise and declare His power.

"O Tower of the flock, the stronghold of the daughter of Zion, unto Thee shall it come, even the first dominion." Micah 4:8. The time has come to which holy men have looked with longing since the flaming sword barred the first pair from Eden, the time for "the redemption of the purchased possession." Ephesians 1:14. The earth originally given to man as his kingdom, betrayed by him into the hands of Satan, and so long held by the mighty foe, has been brought back by the great plan of redemption. All that was lost by sin has been restored. "Thus saith the Lord . . . that formed the earth and made it; He hath established it, He created it not in vain, He formed it to be inhabited." Isaiah 45:18. God's original purpose in the creation of the earth is fulfilled as it is made the eternal abode of the redeemed. "The righteous shall inherit the land, and dwell therein forever." Psalm 37:29.

A fear of making the future inheritance seem too material has led many to spiritualize away the very truths which lead us to look upon it as our home. Christ assured His disciples that He went to prepare mansions for them in the Father's house. Those who accept the teachings of God's word will not be wholly ignorant concerning the heavenly abode. And yet, "eye hath not seen, nor ear heard, neither have entered into the heart of man, the things which God hath prepared for them that love Him." 1 Corinthians 2:9. Human language is inadequate to describe the reward of the righteous. It will be known only to those who behold it. No finite mind can comprehend the glory of the Paradise of God.

In the Bible the inheritance of the saved is called "a country." Hebrews 11:14-16. There the heavenly Shepherd leads His flock to fountains of living waters. The tree of life yields its fruit every month, and the leaves of the tree are for the service of the nations. There are ever-flowing streams, clear as crystal, and beside them waving trees cast their shadows upon the paths prepared for the ransomed of the Lord. There the wide-spreading plains swell into hills of beauty, and the mountains of God rear their lofty summits. On those peaceful plains, beside those living streams, God's people, so long pilgrims and wanderers, shall find a home.

"My people shall dwell in a peaceable habitation, and in sure dwellings, and in quiet resting places." "Violence shall no more be heard in thy land, wasting nor destruction within thy borders; but thou shalt call thy walls Salvation, and thy gates Praise." "They shall build houses, and inhabit them; and they shall plant vineyards, and eat the fruit of them. They shall not build, and another inhabit; they shall not plant, and another eat: ... Mine elect shall long enjoy the work of their hands." Isaiah 32:18; 60:18; 65:21, 22.

There, "the wilderness and the solitary place shall be glad for them; and the desert shall rejoice, and blossom as the rose." "Instead of the thorn shall come up the fir tree, and instead of the brier shall come up the myrtle tree." "The wolf also shall dwell with the lamb, and the leopard shall lie down with the kid; ... and a little child shall lead them." "They shall not hurt nor destroy in all My holy mountain," saith the Lord. Isaiah 35:1; 55:13; 11:6, 9.

Pain cannot exist in the atmosphere of heaven. There will be no more tears, no funeral trains, no badges of mourning. "There shall be no more death, neither sorrow, nor crying: ... for the former things are passed away." "The inhabitant shall not say, I am sick: the people that dwell therein shall be forgiven their iniquity." Revelation 21:4; Isaiah 33:24.

There is the New Jerusalem, the metropolis of the glorified new earth, "a crown of glory in the hand of the Lord, and a royal diadem in the hand of thy God." "Her light was like unto a stone most precious, even like a jasper stone, clear as crystal." "The nations of them which are saved shall walk in the light of it: and the kings of the earth do bring their glory and honor into it." Saith the Lord: "I will rejoice in Jerusalem, and joy in My people." "The tabernacle of God is with men, and He will dwell with them, and they shall be His people, and God Himself shall be with them, and be their God." Isaiah 62:3; Revelation 21:11, 24; Isaiah 65:19; Revelation 21:3.

In the City of God "there shall be no night." None will need or desire repose. There will be no weariness in doing the will of God and offering praise to His name. We shall ever feel the freshness of the morning and shall ever be far from its close. "And they need no candle, neither light of the sun; for the Lord God giveth them light." Revelation 22:5. The light of the sun will be superseded by a radiance which is not painfully dazzling, yet which immeasurably surpasses the brightness of our noontide. The glory of God and the Lamb floods the Holy City with unfading light. The redeemed walk in the sunless glory of perpetual day.

"I saw no temple therein: for the Lord God Almighty and the Lamb are the temple of it." Revelation 21:22. The people of God are privileged to hold open communion with the Father and the Son. "Now we see through a glass, darkly." 1 Corinthians 13:12. We behold the image of God reflected, as in a mirror, in the works of nature and in His dealings with men; but then we shall see Him face to face, without a dimming veil between. We shall stand in His presence and behold the glory of His countenance.

There the redeemed shall know, even as also they are known. The loves and sympathies which God Himself has planted in the soul shall there find truest and sweetest exercise. The pure communion with holy beings, the harmonious social life with the blessed angels and with the faithful ones of all ages who have washed their robes and made them white in the blood of the Lamb, the sacred ties that bind together "the whole family in heaven and earth" (Ephesians 3:15)—these help to constitute the happiness of the redeemed.

There, immortal minds will contemplate with never-failing delight the wonders of creative power, the mysteries of redeeming love. There will be no cruel, deceiving foe to tempt to forgetfulness of God. Every faculty will be developed, every capacity increased. The acquirement of knowledge will not weary the mind or exhaust the energies. There the grandest enterprises may be carried forward, the loftiest aspirations reached, the highest ambitions realized; and still there will arise new heights to surmount, new wonders to admire, new truths to comprehend, fresh objects to call forth the powers of mind and soul and body.

All the treasures of the universe will be open to the study of God's redeemed. Unfettered by mortality, they wing their tireless flight to worlds afar—worlds that thrilled with sorrow at the spectacle of human woe and rang with songs of gladness at the tidings of a ransomed soul. With unutterable delight the children of earth enter into the joy and the wisdom of unfallen beings. They share the treasures of knowledge and understanding gained through ages upon ages in contemplation of God's handiwork. With undimmed vision they gaze upon the glory of creation—suns and stars and systems, all in their appointed order circling the throne of Deity. Upon all things, from the least to the greatest, the Creator's name is written, and in all are the riches of His power displayed.

And the years of eternity, as they roll, will bring richer and still more glorious revelations of God and of Christ. As knowledge is progressive, so will love, reverence, and happiness increase. The more men learn of God, the greater will be their admiration of His character. As Jesus opens before them the riches of redemption and the amazing achievements in the great controversy with Satan, the hearts of the ransomed thrill with more fervent devotion, and with more rapturous joy they sweep the harps of gold; and ten thousand times ten thousand and thousands of thousands of voices unite to swell the mighty chorus of praise.

"And every creature which is in heaven, and on the earth, and under the earth, and such as are in the sea, and all that are in them, heard I saying, Blessing, and honor, and glory, and power, be unto Him that sitteth upon the throne, and unto the Lamb for ever and ever." Revelation 5:13.

The great controversy is ended. Sin and sinners are no more. The entire universe is clean. One pulse of harmony and gladness beats through the vast creation. From Him who created all, flow life and light and gladness, throughout the realms of illimitable space. From the minutest atom to the greatest world, all things, animate and inanimate, in their unshadowed beauty and perfect joy, declare that God is love.

Complete Your Set!

Book One

God's Holy Word

Book Two

America in Prophecy

Book Three

Cracking the Code

Book Four

The World
Out of Control

As the world buckles under the weight of catastrophe—9/11, the great tsunami, earthquakes, forest fires, and wave after wave of hurricanes—this book reveals that these are but a fraction of the destructive forces that are yet to come. With so many crises—the ongoing war on terror; an increase in brutal crimes, especially against children; economic and political instability; lawlessness and confusion; and the proliferation and acceptance of immorality—mainstream, secular media outlets are asking, "Is this the end of the world?"

The key to answering this question is looking into a long-forgotten past. In this classic masterpiece by one of the world's most influential writers, you'll begin to understand the cataclysmic events battering our world in a new light. You'll see how and why history repeats itself, yet more dangerously than in previous times.

So different than anything you've ever read, but authenticated by hundreds of Bible verses and keen insight, This set is an eye-opening journey through human history and beyond that plunges you headfirst into the ultimate battle between good and evil.

Special Edition Complete Series

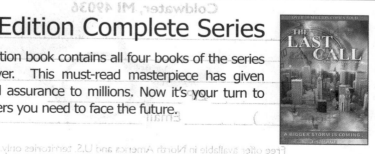

This special edition book contains all four books of the series under one cover. This must-read masterpiece has given knowledge and assurance to millions. Now it's your turn to have the answers you need to face the future.

all Now 1-800-423-1319 or visit www.RemnantPublications.com